# *The Tibetan Book of the Dead*

# The Tibetan Book of the Dead

## The Great Liberation through Hearing

*Modern English translation of the original text*

***Padmasambhava***
(written down by his wife)

*Astrolog Publishing House*

Cover Design: Na'ama Yaffe



ISBN 965-494-201-1

P.O. Box 1123, Hod Hasharon 45111, Israel
Tel: 972-3-9190957
Fax: 972-3-9190958

*www.astrolog.co.il*
*www.astrolog-publishing.co.il*
*www.astrolog-publishing.com*



Published by Astrolog Publishing House 2006

For the purposes of simplicity, the male pronoun is referred to throughout this text.

The **Bardo Thödol**, **The Great Liberation through Hearing** in the bardo that is after death, is one of several guidebooks on six paths for liberation. These include **The Liberation through Hearing**, **The Liberation through Wearing**[1], the **Liberation through Seeing**, **The Liberation through Remembering**, **The Liberation through Tasting**, and **The Liberation through Touching**.

These texts were composed by Padmasambhava and written down, along with other texts, by his wife.

As was common in central Tibet, the texts were buried in various sites across the country. These buried texts are called *termas*—hidden treasures. Padmasambhava granted permission to his best students to discover and reveal these *termas*.

The significance of liberation or release is that every person who comes in contact with **The Great Liberation through Hearing** will experience a sudden flash of illumination when he hears these hidden treasures.

Students of these instructions study the texts until they are totally proficient in them.

This book is a full, modern translation of **The Great Liberation through Hearing**, also known as the **Tibetan Book of the Dead**. It is the central text for Tibetan Buddhists.

It is a difficult text that requires the full attention of the reader. Reading and understanding the text requires great concentration, as well as an understanding of various Buddhist concepts. Some of these will be explained in footnotes.

There are a number of versions of this text in English, but they are written in old-fashioned English that makes understanding these challenging concepts more difficult than necessary. In this edition, we have simplified the language while aiming to maintain the essential meaning and spirit of the original text. We have also included footnotes, to aid the reader in understanding some fundamental concepts in the text.

# Bardo Thödol

Give honor to the gurus[2], the three kayas;

Amitabha[3], the Buddha of limitless light, the dharmakaya[4],
Sambhogakaya[5], the peaceful and wrathful deities, and
Padmasambhava, the protector of beings, the Nirmanakaya[6].

**The Great Liberation through Hearing** is a way of liberation in the bardo[7] for students with average abilities. It is divided into three parts: the introduction, the main subject, and the conclusion.

First of all, the introduction, the means for liberating human beings. First, and while still living, the person must learn and master the instructions for liberating people with very high capabilities. However, if the person is not liberated, he should practice removing himself from consciousness[8]. This will give him spontaneous and automatic liberation when he remembers it, in the bardo of the moment of death.

This should definitely liberate the student with average abilities, but if it doesn't, he should seek assistance through **The Great Liberation through Hearing**, in the bardo of dharmata[9].

In such cases, the yogi[10] should first examine the order of the symptoms of death, as they appear in his own body in the Spontaneous Liberation of the Signs of Death. If he notices all the symptoms of death, then he should apply the exercise to eject his own consciousness. This exercise liberates immediately and spontaneous, the very moment one thinks about it.

If he applies this exercise and ejects himself from consciousness, there is no need to read **The Great Liberation through Hearing**. However, if he does not eject himself from consciousness, then it should be read, clearly and accurately, beside his dead body.

If there is no dead body, the reader should sit on the deceased's chair or bed and declare the Power of Truth. One should think about the dead person's consciousness as one reads, while imagining that the dead person is sitting in front and listening. At this time, it is forbidden to people crying in grief or sadness. For this reason, relatives or members of the deceased's close family must not be in the room.

If the body is present, then in the interval of time between when breathing stops[11] and when the heartbeat stops[12], the deceased person's guru, or one of the guru's students, or a dear friend that was loved and trusted by the deceased loved, should read **The Great Liberation through Hearing** close to his ear.

Now for the instructions on **The Great Liberation through Hearing**. One must make a generous offering to the Three Jewels[13]. If the materials for the generous offering are available, one must declare them. Even if they aren't available, one must imagine a limitless amount of everything to be offered. One must say the **Inspiration Prayer Calling on the Buddhas[14] and Bodhisattvas[15] for Rescue** three, or seven, times.

Afterwards, one must say the inspirational prayer for **Deliverance from the Dangerous Path of the Bardo** and the **Main Verses of the Bardo**. Both of these must be said loudly and distinctly. Afterwards, one must read **The Great Liberation through Hearing** three, or seven, times.

**The Great Liberation through Hearing** is divided into three sections: The first is exposure to bright illumination at the bardo of the moment of death;

the second is the great reminder, the mirroring in the bardo of the dharmata; the third is the instructions for closing the entrance to the womb during the bardo of the coming to life.

First of all, the exposure to the bright illumination in the bardo of the moment of death. By reading these instructions in the ears of the dying person, all sorts of ordinary people will be liberated. This includes people who learnt the teaching, but did not recognize the illumination, despite being intelligent, and people who recognized the light but only practiced it a little bit. With this reading, they will recognize the radiant light, and will skip the experience of the bardo, thereby reaching the dharmakaya stage that hasn't yet appeared.

The method of instruction is as follows:

It is best if the main guru, the person who instructed the person who is about to die, is present. If this is not possible, then one of the students with whom the deceased took the vow of the samaya[16], or a spiritual friend of the same background. If it is impossible to find any of these people, then someone should be found who can read the instruction in a loud voice, accurately and clearly. They must read it several times. The reading will remind the person who is about to die all of the things that his guru taught him. Without a doubt, he will immediately recognize the essential light and be liberated.

The timing of the instruction is as follows: At the moment in which breathing stops, prana[17] sinks into the central nerves of wisdom[18], which is situated in the heart, and the consciousness that is aware will experience the illumination in a natural state[19]. If prana is reversed—if it is thrown backwards and downwards into the right or left nerves, the state of bardo shines for a moment, so the reading of the instructions should take place before the prana returns to the left nerve[20]. This occurs during the length of time it takes to eat a meal[21].

The method of instruction is as follows:

It is best to cause the ejection of the consciousness when the breathing is just about to stop, but if consciousness has not been ejected yet, one can say the following words:

> "Oh noble child [INSERT NAME]!
> The time has come the time for you to find your own path. The moment when your breathing stops, you will see what is called the **Fundamental Illumination**

**of the First Bardo**, something which your guru already revealed to you. This is the dharmata, open and empty. It is like space, an illuminated emptiness, bare and pure consciousness, with no center and no circumference. Recognize it and relax inside of it. I will guide you at the same time."

One must make sure these sentences penetrate into the consciousness of the person who is about to die. To ensure that this occurs, one must repeat them several times, directly into his ears, until he stops breathing. When the last breath is heard, one must lay the deceased onto his right side, in the position of the Sleeping Lion[22], and press firmly on the two arteries that cause sleep, until they stop pulsating. Then the prana that has sunk to the heart cannot leave and it will appear without any doubt through the brahmarandhra[23].

Now the instructions must be read. At this moment, the first bardo, the **Illumination of the Dharmata**, the undistorted consciousness of the dharmakaya, appears in the consciousness of every person. Regular people call this state unconsciousness because the prana sinks during the time between the end of breathing and the end of the beating of the heart. It isn't clear how long this period lasts. That depends upon the spiritual consciousness of the person, and their stage of the yogic training. With sensitive people who have trained a lot and were dedicated to practicing meditation exercises to achieve tranquility, this period lasts a long time. In order to instruct such a person, one must repeat the instructions until pus comes out of the openings in the person's body. As for bad or insensitive people, this period may last no longer than the time it takes to snap one's fingers. For other people, it may take as long as it takes to eat a meal. Since most sutras[24] and tantras[25] say the state of unconsciousness lasts for four and a half days, one should usually strive to expose the illumination for this amount of time.

The method of instruction is as follows: If the dying person is able to recognize the symptoms of death, he will know what to do thanks to the instructions he has already received. However, if he is not able to do this with his own strengths, then his guru, or one of the students of his guru, someone who is also a good friend, will stand close to him and read out loudly and clearly the sequence of the symptoms of death:

> "Now we see the sign that the base of the earth is settling into the water, that the base of the water is dissolving into

the fire, that the base of the fire is fading away into the air, that the base of the air is dissolving into consciousness."

When the sequence is almost complete, one must encourage the dying man and say, "Oh noble child!" or, if he was a guru, "Oh Sir!" "Do not let your thoughts wander." This must be whispered quietly into the ears of the dying man. If there is someone at the side of the dying man, someone who was one of his students or a student of the guru, or another person, that person should call the dying person by name and say to him the following words:

"Oh noble child! That which is called death has arrived at this moment. Accept it with the following approach: 'The hour of my death has arrived. Therefore, at this moment, through this death, I will take on the approach of conscious enlightenment, a state that is friendly and warm, and I will achieve complete enlightenment for the sake of all sentient beings[26], a number which is impossible to count. Through this approach and in this special hour, I will recognize the light of death as the dharmakaya, for the sake of all sentient beings. In this state, when I finally realize the Great Symbol[27], I will act for the benefit of all creatures. Even if I don't achieve this, I will recognize that this is the bardo, when I am unified union with the figure of the Great Symbol in the bardo, I will serve all sentient beings, as limitless as space, in any way that I can.' Don't give up on this approach. Try to remember and implement all of the meditation exercises that you learned in the past."

The following words must be said clearly, with the lips close to the ear of the dying person, in order to remind him of the exercises he should practice, and in order to prevent his concentration from wandering even for a moment. Later on, when the dying man's breathing has stopped completely, one must press firmly on his sleep arteries. If he was a guru, or a spiritual friend who achieved a higher level than yourself, remind him with these words:

"Sir, at this moment, the fundamental illumination is shining above you. Recognize it and rest in your experience in it."

All other people should be guided as follows:

"Oh noble child [INSERT NAME]! Listen! At this moment, the pure light of the dharmata is shining above you. Recognize it. Oh noble child! At this moment, your consciousness is essentially empty and naturally pure. It has no characteristics of existence whatsoever. It has no substance or quality whatsoever, it has no color. Instead, it is empty and pure. This is the dharmata, the female Buddha Samantabhardri[28]. But this emptiness of consciousness is not actually vacant. It is open, sparkling, pure, and full of life. This consciousness is the male Buddha Samantabhardra[29]. These two aspects of your mind, the consciousness whose essence is empty without any content at all, and the consciousness whose essence is full of life and illumination, cannot be separated. That is the dharmakaya of the Buddha. Your consciousness is emptiness and illumination that are inseparable. The form is a great quantity of light, a light that has no beginning and no end. Therefore, it is the Buddha of Absolute Light. All you have to do is know this and identify it. As soon as you recognize that the fundamental nature of your consciousness is the Buddha, your ability to see into your consciousness will rest inside the consciousness of the Buddha."

Repeat this clearly and precisely three, or seven, times. First of all, this will remind the deceased of what his guru revealed to him in the past. Second of all, the deceased will recognize his own shining consciousness. Third of all, he will be united with the dharmakaya the moment when he recognizes himself. Without any doubt, he will be liberated.

If he recognizes the first illumination, he will become liberated. However, if there is any fear that he didn't recognize his first illumination, than a second illumination will appear. This will occur after a little more time has past, after he has stopped breathing. This takes the same length of time as it takes to eat a meal.

The prana enters the right or left nerve; this depends upon whether the karma is good or bad. The prana then leaves the body through one of the body's openings and consciousness suddenly becomes clear.

The length of time that this takes varies, and depends upon whether the deceased is sensitive or not, and whether he has practiced the teachings or not. It may last for as long as it takes to eat a meal. In this case, his consciousness comes out, and he does not know if he is alive or dead. He will hear the sounds of the family that has gathered around him just as he heard before, and he will hear their cries, as well.

It is during this time, before the confusion and violence of the images of karma appear, and before there are fears of the Angel of Death, that one must give the instructions. Here, there is a distinction between the **Completion Stage**[30] and the **Generation Stage**[31]. If the deceased was working on the **Completion Stage**, one must call his name three times and repeat the instructions described above regarding illumination. If the deceased was working on the **Generation Stage**, one must read the sadhana[32] and the description of his yidam[33] out loud and remind the deceased with the following words:

"Oh noble child! Meditate on your yidam and don't let yourself be distracted. Concentrate totally on your yidam. Imagine him as a figure that has no presence of his own, just as the moon reflects itself in the water. Do not imagine it as something that has a solid shape or physical form."

If the deceased is a regular person, guide him with the following words: "Mediate on the Buddha of Great Compassion."

There is no doubt that, if the deceased didn't recognize the bardo until now, he will understand it after he has been guided in this manner. However, if he is not trained in meditation, even if his guru revealed it to him while he was still living, he cannot distinguish the state of the bardo with his own powers. In such a case, his guru, or one of the guru's students, will have to show it to him. In the same way, someone has to guide people who cannot remember what they learnt before during the bardo of the moment of death because they have been confused by of a serious illness, despite the fact that they may be skilled in meditation. Likewise, it is very important to guide people that are likely to enter lower levels of existence, despite having previous experience meditating, because they have broken promises or rules, or because they stopped practicing their samaya.

Of course, it is best when the deceased understands during the first bardo. However, if he doesn't understand, this reminder, spoken in the second bardo, can awaken his insight and then he will be liberated.

During the second bardo, his body is now in the nature known as the Pure Illusory Body[34]. Whereas before he didn't know if he was alive or dead, his consciousness suddenly becomes clear. If he understands the instructions at this stage, a meeting occurs between the Illumination of the Mother[35] and the Illumination of the Son[36]. At this moment, the deceased is no longer ruled by his karma. Just as the light of the sun overpowers the darkness, so too does the Illumination of the Path overpower the strength of the karma and the deceased achieves liberation. The second stage of the bardo appears before the mental body. His consciousness can hear again, just as it did before. If the deceased understands the instructions at this stage, the goal is achieved. The confused rays of the karma haven't appeared yet and the deceased can go wherever he wants.

In this manner, the deceased is liberated in the second bardo by recognizing the illumination. This occurs even if he didn't recognize the fundamental illumination. However, if he hasn't been liberated by this point, the third bardo appears. This is the bardo of dharmata. Confusing images of karma appear in the third bardo, so it is very important to that the instructions of the bardo of dharamta are read and shown to the deceased at this moment, as this is very powerful and effective.

Right now, his family will be crying heavily. They are setting aside food for him and they have taken off his clothes. His bed has been broken into pieces or removed, and other similar acts are being carried out. The deceased sees them and their actions, but they cannot see him. He hears that they are calling his name, but they cannot hear that he is calling back to them. So, in despair, he continues along his path.

Three things will appear at this time: sounds, colorful lights, and rays of light. Fear of these phenomena will cause the deceased to feel weak, scared, bewildered. At his moment, one must read the instructions of the bardo of dharmata. One must call the deceased by name and say these words very clearly:

"Oh noble child! Pay attention to what I am saying and don't allow yourself to be distracted. There are six stages of bardo: the bardo of birth, the bardo of dreams, the bardo of samadhi-meditation[37], the bardo of the moment of death, the bardo of dharmata, and the bardo of becoming. Oh noble child! You will experience three stages of bardo: the bardo of the moment of death, the bardo of dharmata, and the bardo of becoming. Among these three bardo, the illumination of the dharmata in the bardo of the moment of death shined on you until yesterday, but you didn't recognize it. Therefore, you must wander here. At this moment, you will experience the bardo of the dharamata and the bardo of becoming, so recognize what I am about to reveal to you. Pay attention and don't allow yourself to be distracted.

"Oh noble child! That which is known as death has arrived. You are not the only person to leave this world; it happens to everyone. Don't desire this life. Don't feel a yearning for it. Even if you have these feelings, you won't be able to stay here. All you can do is wander in samsara[38]. Don't yearn. Don't desire. Remember the Three Jewels. Oh noble child! It doesn't matter what scary projections will appear in the bardo of dharmata. Don't forget these words. Continue to move forward and remember their meaning. The most important thing for you to do is use them to recognize:

> Now, when the bardo of the dharmata
>   shines on me,
> I will leave behind all of my fears,
> May I recognize everything that appears,
> In the projections of my consciousness.
> And I will know that this is a vision of
>   the bardo.
> At this moment, when I have reached
>   the level of consciousness,
> May I not be afraid of the tranquil and
>   furious deities,
> As these are really images that have
>   been projected from my own mind.

"Continue to go forward and say these words clearly and precisely. Remember what they mean. Don't forget them, because the most important thing is to recognize what occurs with certainty. Everything may seem extremely frightening, but remember that they are nothing more than images that you have projected yourself.

"Oh noble child! When your body separates from your consciousness, the dharmata appears. Although is pure and clear, it can be hard to identify. It is bright and shining, indeed, it has a frightening brightness. It sparkles like an mirage on flat lands in the spring. Don't be afraid of it and don't be confused. It is the natural brightness of your own dharmata, so recognize it.

"From inside the light, you'll hear the sounds of great thunder. The sound is as strong as the noise from a thousand claps of thunder. Don't be afraid. This is the sound of your dharmata. What you have now is a mental body of unconscious inclinations. You have no flesh and you have no blood, so don't be afraid. Whatever sounds you hear, whatever colors and rays of lights you see, none of them can hurt you. You cannot die. All you have to do is recognize them as images that have been projected from your own mind. This is the bardo state.

"Oh noble child! If you don't recognize all these phenomena as projections of yourself, it doesn't matter what exercises in meditation you did in your life. If you don't come to this awareness, the colorful lights will frighten you. You'll be confused by the sounds and terrified by the rays of light. If you don't understand this fundamental issue, you won't recognize the sounds and lights and rays, and you'll continue to wander in samsara.

"Oh noble child! After being unconscious for four and a half days, you'll move on. You'll wake up from your faint and ask yourself what happened. At this moment, recognize the state of bardo. At this moment in the samara there will be a complete reversal. Everything will seem to you to be lights and images.

"Everything around you will glow with a blue light, and the Blessed Vairocana will appear before you. He comes from the Central Realm of the All Pervading Circle. His body is white and he sits on a throne that is shaped like a lion. In his hand, he holds a wheel with eight spokes. He hugs his mate, the Queen of Vajra Space.

"The blue light of the skandha[39] of consciousness will come towards you, with its fundamental purity. The wisdom of the dharmadhatu[40], shining and clear, piercing and brilliant, will penetrate from the heart of the Vairocana and his mate, and will come to you, shining in your eyes until you cannot see. At the very same moment, the white light of the devas[41] will also approach you, penetrating into you.

“At that moment, because you are being influenced by bad karma, you’ll be very frightened. You’ll try to hide from the wisdom of the dharmadhatu and the shining blue light. At the same time, a feeling awaken inside of you, a feeling of pleasure toward the white light of devas.

“Don’t be scared or confused by the bright, sharp, and clear light of Supreme Wisdom. This is the ray of light of the Buddha. It is called the wisdom of dharmadhatu. Follow it with faith and longing. Pray to it, and think to yourself, ‘This ray of light is the compassion of the Blessed Vairocana. I will find shelter in it.’

“It is the Blessed Vairocana that has come to invite you along the dangerous path of the bardo. This is the ray of light of the compassion of Vairocana.

“Don’t indulge yourself in the pleasure of the white light of the devas. Don’t be drawn toward it and don’t desire it. If you allow yourself to be attracted to this light, you’ll wander in the realms of the devas, you’ll drift between six types of existence. This blocks your ability to be liberated, so don’t look at it, not even briefly. Only look at the clear blue light, concentrate only on the Blessed Vairocana, and say this inspirational prayer:

"When I wander in samsara,
Due to my great stupidity,
In the path of the shining light,
Of the wisdom of dharmadhatu,
May the Blessed Vairocana lead me,
And may his mate, the Queen of Vajra
  Space,
Protect me from behind.
May they help me to cross,
The bardo's dangerous path,
And bring me to the perfect Buddha
  state."

If this prayer is said with deep conviction, the deceased will dissolve into a rainbow of light in the heart of the Blessed Vairocana and his mate. He will turn into a Sambhogakaya Buddha in the Central Realm of the Crowded.

Despite this guidance, however, the deceased may still be frightened by the lights and rays. This may be because of the power of his own anger, or because of karma that is blocking his mind. The deceased may escape, and may be confused even after saying this prayer. In such cases, Vajrasattva's deities will come on the second day to invite him, along with his bad karma, to hell. Therefore, in order to guide him, one must say the following words:

"Oh noble child! Pay attention to what I am saying and don't allow yourself to be distracted. On the second day, everything around you will glow with a white light—water in its pure form. Along with it, the Blessed Vajrasattva-Aksobhhay will appear before you. He comes from the blue Eastern Realm of Complete Joy. His body is blue and he sits on a throne that is shaped like an elephant. In his hand, he holds a five-pointed vajra[42]. He hugs his mate, Buddha-Locana. Two male Bodhisattvas are with him—Ksitigrabha and Maitreya. He also has two female Bodhisattvas with him—Lasya and Puspa. In total, you will see six Buddha forms in front of you.

"The white light of the skandha of form will come towards you, with its fundamental purity. The reflective wisdom, shining white, clear and brilliant, will approach you from the heart of the Vajrasattva and his mate. It will shine in your eyes, so that you cannot see. At the very same moment, along with the light of wisdom, the dim smoky light of the creatures from hell will also approach you, penetrating into you.

"At that moment, because you are being influenced by bad karma, you'll be very frightened. You'll try to escape from the bright white light. At the same time, the dim, smoky light of the creatures from hell will seem desirable to you.

“Don’t be afraid of the penetrating white, shining and clear light. Recognize that it is wisdom. Follow it with faith and longing. Pray to it, and think to yourself, ‘This ray of light is the compassion of the Blessed Vajrasattva. I will find shelter in it.’

“It is the Blessed Vajrasattva that has come to invite you, and to save your from the dangers of the bardo. This is the ray of light of the compassion of Vajrasattva, so feel yourself drawn to it.

“Don’t indulge in the dim and smoky light of the creatures from hell. This is the inviting path of the bad karma that has accumulated as a result of your own anger. It is inviting you to follow. If you continue along this path, you will fall into hell, you will sink into a swamp of misery and hard suffering. From this hell, there is no escape. This obstacle prevents you from walking towards liberation, so don’t even glance at it. Stop being angry. Don’t proceed toward it and don’t be drawn to it. Feel longing toward the white light, the bright and shining light. Say this inspirational prayer while concentrating wholeheartedly on the Blessed Vajrasattva:

When I wander in samsara,
Due to my great anger,
In the path of the shining light,
Of the wisdom of the image in the
mirror,
May the Blessed Vajrasattva lead
me,
And may his mate, Buddha-
Locana,
Protect me from behind.
May they help me to cross,
The bardo's dangerous path,
And bring me to the perfect
Buddha state."

If this prayer is said with deep conviction, the deceased will dissolve into a rainbow of light in the heart of the Blessed Vajrasattva and his mate, and turn into a Sambhogakaya Buddha in the Eastern Realm of Complete Joy.

Despite this guidance, however, some people are still frightened by the hook of the light of compassion. This may be because of bad karma or because of their pride, and so they try to escape. In such cases, the Blessed Ratnasambhava will appear on the third day, with his entourage of deities, along with the path of light from the world of humans, in order to invite him. In order to guide him again, one must call out the name of the deceased and say the following words:

"Oh noble child! Pay attention to what I am saying and don't allow yourself to be distracted. On the third day, everything around you will glow with a yellow light— earth in its pure form. The Blessed Ratnasambhava will appear, from the yellow Southern Realm of The Glorious. His body is yellow and he sits on a throne that is in the shape of a horse. In his hand, he holds a jewel that grants wishes. He hugs his mate, Makami. Two male Bodhisattvas are with him—Akasagarbha and Samantabhadra. Two female Bodhisattvas—Mala and Dhupa—are also with him. In total, you will see six Buddha forms in front of you.

"The yellow light of the skandha of feeling will come towards you, with its fundamental purity. The wisdom of equality, shining yellow, clear and brilliant, will approach you from the heart of the Ratnasambhava and his mate. It will shine in your eyes, so that you cannot see. At the very same moment, along with the light of wisdom, the dim blue light of humans will also approach you, penetrating into you.

"At that moment, because you are being influenced by your pride, you will be filled with fear. You'll try to escape from the bright yellow light. At the same time, the dim, blue light of humans will seem desirable to you.

"Don't be afraid of the penetrating yellow, shining, and clear light. Recognize that it is wisdom. Let your mind rest, relax, and enjoy being inactive. Allow your mind to be drawn to it.

"Recognize that this is the natural radiance of your mind. If you do this, all the forms and lights and rays will merge with you, even if you don't feel devotion and even if you don't say the inspiration prayer. Then you will attain enlightenment.

"If you cannot recognize that this is the natural radiance of your mind, pray to it by thinking to yourself, 'This ray of light is the compassion of the Blessed Ratnasambhava. I will find shelter in it.' It is the hook of the compassion of the Blessed Ratnasambhava, so yearn for it.

"Don't indulge in the dim blue light of humans. This is the inviting and brightened path of your unconscious inclinations. It is created by your immense pride. If you continue along this path, you will fall into the human cycle. You will experience birth, old age, death, and suffering. You will never escape from the swamp of samsara. This obstacle prevents you from walking toward liberation, so don't look at it, not even for a moment. Stop being proud. Put an end to your unconscious inclinations. Don't be drawn to this and don't yearn for it. Long for the bright yellow light and say this inspiration prayer, while concentrating wholeheartedly on the Blessed Ratnasambhava:

When I wander in samsara,
Due to my intense pride,
In the path of the shining light,
Of the wisdom of equality,
May the Blessed Ratnasambhava lead
  me,
And may his mate, Mamaki,
Protect me from behind.
May they help me to cross,
The bardo's dangerous path,
And bring me to the perfect Buddha
  state."

If this prayer is said with deep conviction, the deceased will dissolve into a rainbow of light in the heart of the Blessed Ratnasambhava and his mate, and become a Sambhogakaya Buddha in the Southern Realm of The Glorious.

Liberation is certain after being shown in this manner, even for the weakest person. Despite this guidance, however, people who have run out of luck, or people who have done terrible things, or people who have not practiced their samaya, may not recognize and be liberated. These people may be afraid of the lights and sounds, they may be distracted by desire, and by the obstructions that were created by their bad karma.

In such cases, the Blessed Amitabha will appear with his entourage of deities on the fourth day, to invite the deceased down the path of light of hungry ghosts, built from desire and cruelty. In order to guide him again, one must call out the name of the deceased and say the following words:

"Oh noble child! Pay attention to what I am saying and don't allow yourself to be distracted. On the fourth day, everything around you will glow with a red light—fire in its pure form. The Blessed Amitabha will appear, from the red Western Realm of The Blissful. His body is red and he sits on a throne that is in the shape of a peacock. In his hand, he holds a lotus. He hugs his mate, Pandaravasini. Two male Bodhisattvas are with him—Avalokitesvara and Mañjusri. Two female Bodhisattvas—Gita and Aloka—are also with him. In total, you will see six Buddha forms in front of you.

"The red light of the skandha of perception will come towards you, with its fundamental purity. The wisdom of discrimination, shining red, decorated with orbs of light, clear and brilliant, sharp and shining, will approach you from the heart of the Amitabha and his mate. They will shine in your eyes, so that you cannot see.

"Don't be afraid of it. At the very same moment, along with the light of wisdom, the dim yellow light of hungry ghosts will also approach you. Don't indulge in it. Give up your desire and yearning.

"At that moment, because of your intense desire, you will be filled with fear. You'll try to escape from the bright red light. At the same time, the dim yellow light of the hungry ghosts will seem desirable to you. Don't be afraid of the penetrating red, shining, and clear light. Recognize that it is wisdom. Let your mind rest, relax, and enjoy being inactive. Allow your mind to be drawn to it faithfully and with longing.

"Recognize that this is the natural radiance of your mind. If you do this, all the forms and lights and rays will merge with you, even if you don't feel devotion and don't say the inspirational prayer. Then you will attain enlightenment.

“If you cannot recognize that this is the natural radiance of your mind, pray to it by thinking to yourself, ‘This ray of light is the compassion of the Blessed Amitabha. I will find shelter in it.’ It is the hook of the compassion of the Blessed Amitabha, so yearn for it. Be devoted to it, do not try to escape. Even if you try to escape, it will stay with you anyway.

“Don’t be afraid. Don’t be drawn to the dim yellow light of hungry ghosts. This is the path of unconscious inclinations. It has been created by your intense desire. If you allow yourself to be drawn to it, you will fall into the world of hungry ghosts. You will be miserable. You will be unbearably hungry and thirsty. This obstacle prevents you from walking toward liberation, so don’t allow yourself to be attracted to it. Give up your unconscious inclinations.

Don’t be drawn to it, don’t yearn for it. Long for the bright red light and say this inspirational prayer while concentrating wholeheartedly on the Blessed Amitabha and his mate:

> When I wander in samsara,
> Due to my strong desire,
> In the path of the shining light,
> Of the wisdom of discrimination,

May the Blessed Amitabha lead me,
And may his mate, Pandaravasini,
Protect me from behind.
May they help me to cross,
The bardo's dangerous path,
And bring me to the perfect Buddha
state."

If this prayer is said with deep conviction, the deceased he will dissolve into a rainbow of light in the heart of the Blessed Amitabha, Infinite Light, and his mate, and become a Sambhogakaya Buddha in the Western Realm of The Blissful.

Still, it is possible that liberation won't occur after this. Unconscious inclinations may be hard to give up after a long time, and people who are affected by jealousy or really bad karma may still be afraid of the sounds and lights. They may still be free from the hook of compassion. These people will continue to wander downwards, toward the fifth day of the bardo state.

In such cases, the entourage of deities of the Blessed Amoghasiddhi will appear on the fifth day, to invite them down the bright path of the jealous deities, built from envy. In order to guide the deceased once again, one must call out his name and say the following words:

"Oh noble child! Pay attention to what I am saying and don't allow yourself to be distracted. On the fifth day, everything around you will glow with a green light—air in its pure form. At the same time, the Blessed Amoghasiddhi, the head of the circle, will appear, from the green Northern Realm of Performance. His body is green and he sits on a throne in the shape of shang-shang birds[43] soaring in the sky. In his hand, he holds a double vajra. He hugs his mate, Samaya-Tara. Two male Bodhisattvas are with him—Vajrapani and Sarvanivarana-viskambhin. Two female Bodhisattvas—Gandha and Naivedya—are also with him. In total, you will see six Buddha forms in front of you.

"The green light of the skandha of perception will come towards you, with its fundamental purity. The wisdom of performance, shining green, bright and clear, sharp and frightening, decorated with orbs of light, will approach you from the heart of the Amoghasiddhi and his mate. It will penetrate into your heart. It will shine into your eyes so that you cannot see.

"Don't be afraid. It is the spontaneous play of your mind. Relax in the state you are in, free from activity and worry, where there is no such thing as near or far, love or hate.

"At the very same moment, along with the light of wisdom, the dim red light of the jealous deities, caused by envy, will also approach you. Meditate so that you feel no difference between love and hate. If your intelligence cannot stand it, simply refuse to indulge in it.

"At that moment, because of your intense envy, you will be filled with fear. You'll try to escape from the sharp green light. At the same time, the dim red light of the jealous deities will seem desirable to you. Don't be afraid of the penetrating green light. Recognize that it is wisdom. Let your mind rest, relax, and enjoy being inactive.

"Pray to it by thinking, 'This ray of light is the compassion of the Blessed Amoghasiddhi. I will find shelter in it.' It is the hook of the compassion of the Blessed Amoghasiddhi, it is named for its Performance wisdom, so yearn for it and do not try to escape. Even if you try to escape, it will stay with you anyway.

"Don't be afraid. Don't be drawn to the dim red light of jealous deities. This is the inviting path made from bad karma that has been created by your intense envy.

If you allow yourself to be drawn to it, you will fall into the world of jealous deities. You will be unbearably miserable from fighting. This obstacle prevents you from walking toward liberation, so don't be attracted to it. Give up your unconscious inclinations.

Long for the bright green light and say this inspirational prayer while concentrating wholeheartedly on the Blessed Amoghasiddhi and his mate:

When I wander in samsara,
Due to my intense envy,
In the path of the shining light,
Of the wisdom of performance,
May the Blessed Amoghasiddhi
  lead me,
And may his mate, Samaya-Tara,
Protect me from behind.
May they help me to cross,
The bardo's dangerous path,
And bring me to the perfect
Buddha state."

If this prayer is said with deep conviction, the deceased will dissolve into a rainbow of light in the heart of the Blessed Amoghasiddhi and his mate, and become a Sambhogakaya Buddha in the Northern Realm of Performance.

Regardless of how weak a person's karma may be, it is impossible not to be liberated after being shown this. However, a person who is used to having strong desires, a person who is not familiar with the pure visions of wisdom, may nevertheless be led backwards by his own evil desires.

The light of compassion may not be able to catch such a person. He may be confused and afraid of the lights and sounds. He may continue to wander backwards. In such a case, the Buddhas of all five families, along with their mates and attendants, will appear at the same time, and the lights from all six realms will shine simultaneously. In order to guide him again, one must call out the name of the deceased and say the following words:

"Oh noble child! Pay attention to what I am saying and don't allow yourself to be distracted. Until yesterday, you were shown the light of each of the five families. However, because of your bad inclinations, you were confused by these lights. Rather than be liberated, you have remained where you are.

"If you had recognized that these natural wisdoms are images that were projected from your thoughts, you would have dissolved into a rainbow of light in one of the five families and become a Sambhogakaya Buddha. However, because you didn't recognize any of them, you are still wandering. Now you must watch and pay close attention.

"All five families will appear at the same time, and the four wisdoms will shine on you at once. They are coming to invite you—recognize them. Oh noble child! The four colored lights, of the four pure elements, will shine at the same moment. At the same time, the Buddha Vairocana and his mate will appear, from the Central Realm of the All Pervading Circle, and the Buddha Vajrasattva and his mate will appear, from the Eastern Realm of Complete Joy, and the Buddha Ratnasambhava and his mate will appear, from the Southern Realm of The Glorious, and the Buddha Amitabha and his mate will appear, from the Western Realm of The Blissful, and the Buddha Amoghasiddhi will appear, from the Northern Realm of Performance, out of the space of the rainbow of light.

"Oh noble child! The angry male guardians of the gates will also appear, in a circle around these Buddhas. Vijaya, the victorious one, Yamantaka, the destroyer of death, Hayagriva, the king with the neck of a horse, and Amrtakundali, with the urn of nectar. The female guardians of the gates will also appear. These are Ankusa with the hook, Pasa with the noose, Srnkhala with the chain, and Ghanta with the bell. The six blessed sages will also appear. These are: Indra of the hundred sacrifices, the sage of the deities; Vemacitra of the splendid robe, the sage of the jealous deities; the Lion of the Sakyas, the sage of humans; Dhruvasinha, the steadfast lion, the sage of the animals; Jvalamukha of the flaming mouth, the sage of the hungry ghosts; and Dharmaraja, the dharma king, the sage of the creatures from hell. Samantabhadra and Samantabhadri, the All-Good Father and Mother of all the Buddhas, will also appear. In total, forty-two deities of the Sambhogakay will come from your heart. They are the pure form of images that you have projected. They will appear before you, so recognize them.

"Oh noble child! Those realms lie only within the four areas of your own heart. They do not exist anywhere else. The fifth realm is the center. These images come directly from your heart. They are the natural, spontaneous projections of your mind, so recognize them as they are. Oh noble child! These images aren't too small or too big. They are the perfect size. Each one has its own decorations, clothes, colors, stature, throne and symbol. They are spread out in five pairs. Each pair is surrounded by five colored lights. The complete mandala[44] will appear at once, with all of the male and female deities. Recognize them, as they are your yidams.

"Oh noble child! The light rays of the four Wisdoms will shine from the hearts of those Buddhas onto your own heart. They will be fine and clear, like sunbeams.

"First, the wisdom of the dharmadhatu. This will come from the heart of Vairocana. It will be a cloth of bright white rays, brilliant and frightening. It contains a sparkling white disc within it. The disc is clear and bright, like a mirror facing downwards. This mirror is decorated with five smaller discs, and these are decorated with more discs, smaller discs, so that it actually has no center or circumference.

"A cloth of bright blue light, the light of mirror like wisdom, will come from the heart of Vajrasattva. Within it there is a blue disc, like a turquoise bowl facing downwards. This bowl is decorated with smaller discs.

"A cloth of bright yellow light, the light of equality wisdom, will come from the heart of Ratnasambhava.

Within it there is a yellow disc, like a golden bowl facing downwards. This bowl is decorated with smaller discs.

"A cloth of bright red light, the light of the wisdom to distinguish, will come from the heart of Amitabha. Within it there is a sparkling red disc, like a coral bowl facing downwards. This bowl is decorated with five smaller discs, and these are decorated with more discs, smaller discs, so that it actually has no center or circumference.

"These will also shine on your heart.

"Oh noble child! These images are the natural, spontaneous projections of your mind. They haven't come from any other place. Don't be attracted to them. Don't be frightened by them. Stay calm and allow your mind to stay free of thoughts. Once you are in this state, the images and light rays will merge, and you can reach enlightenment.

"Oh noble child! The green light of performance wisdom will not appear, because the energy of your wisdom isn't ready yet.

"Oh noble child! This is the experience of the four combined wisdoms. This is the path of the

Vajrasattva. When you see these images, you must remember the instructions you received from your guru. If you remember the meanings, you will have faith in earlier experiences and recognize them. It will be like the meeting between a mother and son, or like seeing old friends. By eliminating any doubt, you will recognize these images, and proceed along the pure, constant path of the dharmata. From this, a constant state of meditation will arise. You will merge into the great self-existing form of wisdom and become a Sambhogakaya Buddha. From this point, there is no return.

"Oh noble child! The lights of the six false realms will shine together with the lights of wisdom. These are the dim white light of the devas, the dim red light of the jealous deities, the dim blue light of humans, the dim green light of animals, the dim yellow light of the hungry ghosts, and the dim smoky light of the creatures from hell. These six lights will shine at the same time as the lights of pure wisdom are shining. Do not be attracted to these lights. Stay calm and keep your mind free of thoughts. If you fear pure wisdom, and if you allow yourself to be drawn to the impure lights of the six realms, you will take on a creature's body, and you will become weary. You will never have any escape from the ocean of misery of samsara.

"Oh noble child! You will be afraid of these images of lights of pure wisdom if you haven't been shown by a guru. You will be attracted to the impure lights of the samsara. Don't let this happen! Be devoted to the sharp and bright lights of pure wisdom. Think to yourself devotedly, 'The rays of light of wisdom and compassion of the Blessed Ones have come to get me. I will take shelter in them.' Do not let yourself be attracted to the lights of the six realms of illusion.

Say this inspirational prayer and concentrate on the Buddhas of the five families and their mates:

When I wander through,
The five poisons in samsara,
On the bright path of the four wisdoms,
May the victorious conquerors, the five
  families, lead me,
And may the mates of the five families
  be behind me.
And may they save me from the bright
  paths,
Of the six impure realms.
May they help me to cross,
The bardo's dangerous path,
And bring me to the five pure Buddha
  realms."

When a superior person says this inspirational prayer, he recognizes the images he has projected in his own mind. He merges with his inner self and becomes a Buddha. The average person recognizes the images projected through devotion, and becomes liberated. Even the lowest person can prevent rebirth in the six realms by purifying himself through prayer and understanding the combined meaning of the four wisdoms. Through this, he can achieve enlightenment by the path of Vajrasattva. Many sentient beings will recognize and be liberated by being shown in this clear and precise manner.

Still, some inferior people will not recognize this, even when it is shown to them clearly. These people may be from uncivilized places; they may be evil people with no experience in dharma[45]; they may also be people who have neglected their samaya practice. These people will be confused by their karma, and will continue to walk backwards.

In such cases, the vidyadharas[46] will come from the Pure Realm of Space and invite them. At the same time, the bright path of the animals, produced from emotions of ignorance, will come to meet them. At this moment, one must call the deceased by name and say the following words:

"Oh noble child! Pay attention to what I am saying and don't allow yourself to be distracted. On the seventh day, a pure, multicolored light will shine in your mind. The vidyadharas will come from the Pure Realm of Space to invite you.

"The vidyadhara known as the Unsurpassable Fully Developed, the Lotus Lord of the Dance, will appear in a mandala filled with multicolored lights. His body is bright with color and he will embrace his mate, the Red Dakini[47]. He will dance and gesture, he will gaze at the sky. He will hold a knife in the shape of a crescent and a skull full of blood.

"The vidyadhara known as Established in the Stages will appear from the east of the mandala. His body is white, and he has a radiant smile. He embraces his mate, the White Dakini, and dances, gesturing and gazing at the sky, with a crescent knife and a skull full of blood.

"The vidyadhara known as the Lord of Life will appear from the south of the mandala. His body is yellow, and he has a beautiful shape. He embraces his mate, the Yellow Dakini, and dances, gesturing and gazing at the sky, with a crescent knife and a skull full of blood.

"The vidyadhara known as the Great Symbol will appear from the west of the mandala. His body is red, and he has a radiant smile. He embraces his mate, the Red Dakini, and dances, gesturing and gazing at the sky, with a crescent knife and a skull full of blood.

"The vidyadhara known as the Spontaneously Arisen will appear from the west of the mandala. His body is green, and he is both angry and happy. He embraces his mate, the Green Dakini, and dances, gesturing and gazing at the sky, with a crescent knife and a skull full of blood.

"There will be countless dakinis around these vidyadharas. There will be dakinis from burial areas and dakinis from the four families. There will be dakinis from the three worlds, the ten directions, and the twenty-four pilgrimage sites.

"There will be male and female warriors, servants, and protectors of dharma. They will wear decorates made from six bones. They will carry drums and trumpets made from thigh bones. They will carry drums made of skulls and banners made from the skins of children. They will carry canopies and ribbons made from human skins. They will burn incense that is made from human flesh. They will have countless types of musical instruments, and they will make so much noise that they fill every corner of the universe, causing it to shake and tremble. The vibrations of their music will be so great they will cause one's head to split. They will dance all sorts of dances, and invite people who have practiced samaya to participate. They will punish people who have neglected it.

"Oh noble child! In this unconscious realm, pure wisdom will shine with five colored lights, like colored threads that are twisted together. The lights will flash, vibrate, and shimmer. They are bright and clear, sharp and terrifying. They will come from the hearts of the five vidyadharas, and they will penetrate deep into your heart, so that you cannot bear to look at it. At the very same moment, along with the light of wisdom, the dim green light of the animals will also approach you, penetrating into you. Because of your unconscious inclinations, you will be confused. You will be filled with fear and you will try to escape from the five-colored light. At the same time, the dim green light of the animals will seem desirable to you. Don't be afraid of the bright five-colored light. Recognize that it is wisdom.

"You will hear the sound of a thousand claps of thunder from within the light. That is the spontaneous sound of the dharma. The sound is powerful and reverberates. It is a penetrating sound of war-cries and angry mantras. Do not fear this sound and do not try to escape from it. Recognize that it simply a projection from your own mind.

"Don't allow yourself to be attracted to the dim green light of the animals. Do not be attracted to it, for if you are, you will fall into the ignorance that exists in the animal realm. You will experience the great suffering of stupidity, dumbness and slavery. There is no escape from this suffering, so don't allow yourself to be drawn to it.

"Instead, feel yourself drawn to the bright and clear five-color light. Concentrate wholeheartedly on the blessed vidyadharas, the divine teachers. Think to yourself: 'These vidyadharas have come to me with warriors and dakinis. They are here to invite me to the Pure Realm of Space. Think about sentient beings, such as myself, who are not worthy, and who have not been taken, even though so many deities of the five families of Buddhas have reached out to them. How it is to be me! May all the vidyadharas grab me with their hooks of compassion, and not let me sink any lower. May they pull me up quickly to the Pure Realm of Space.'

"Concentrate deeply and say this inspirational prayer:

May the divine vidyadharas think about me,
And lead me along with the path with great love.
When I wander in samsara,
Due to my intense inclinations,
Along the bright path,
Of innate wisdom,
May the vidyadharas and warriors lead me,
And may their mates, the dakinis, be behind me.
And may they help me to cross,
The bardo's dangerous path,
And bring me to the Pure Realm of Space."

If this prayer is said with deep conviction, the deceased will dissolve into a rainbow of light in the heart of the divine vidyadharas, and be born into the Pure Realm of Space. There is no doubt about this. All spiritual friends recognize at this stage and will be liberated. Even those with bad inclinations will be liberated at this stage.

This is the end of the first part of **The Great Liberation through Hearing**. It is concerned with recognizing the Light of Wisdom during the bardo of the moment of death, and during the peaceful bardo of the dharmata.

Now the appearance of the bardo of the furious deities will be explained.

Until now, there were the seven stages in the bardo of the peaceful deities. The deceased has had many chances to recognize one of the stages, and many opportunities to achieve liberation during these stages. However, there are many sentient beings, and bad karma can be strong. For some people, consciousness lasts for a long time and the obstruction of bad karma are hard to see through. These people will not be liberated during those seven stages. They will continue to wander downwards, confused and ignorant, even though they have been shown the way.

After the peaceful deities, the vidyadharas, and the dakinis have appeared, the peaceful deities will turn into fifty-eight fiery and furious deities. The deities are different now. This is the bardo of the furious deities, and the deities are difficult to recognize—and terrifying. One has no control over one's own thoughts, one feels dizzy and faint. Even a little recognition will lead to liberation in this bardo, because a person is so frightened he has no time to be distracted.

If one cannot recognize at this point, then nothing will help, not even an ocean of learning. Even great teachers and philosophers may be confused at this stage. They will continue wandering in samsara. Ordinary people may feel intense fear and may run away. If they do this, they will become deeply miserable. Nevertheless, a tantric yogin[48], even the lowest of the low, will recognize the blood-drinking deities as yidams when he sees them. He will trust them as he trusts old friends, and he will join with them to become a Buddha. He will have meditated on these blood-drinking deities during life, so when he sees them later, he will recognize and become liberated.

However, teachers and great philosophers, who followed religious rules and were highly trained in human words and learning, may not see any of the signs they expect to see in death, such as rainbows (from funeral pyres) or relics. They didn't believe in the tantras when they lived—they mocked them—and so they won't recognize them in the bardo. When they see something new, they will consider it an enemy. They will feel hostility toward it and continue downward. Even if these philosophers were wise in their life, they did not practice tantras, so signs that they expect to see such as rainbows and relics will not appear.

Any person who did believe in the tantras—even the lowest type of person, the most uncultured and coarsest individual—will be liberated at this point. Even if he didn't practice the tantras, the fact that he believed in them and had faith in them is enough for him to be liberated. He will see some sign—a rainbow or a relic—because the power of tantric teaching is that great.

Exceptional tantric yogins, those who really practiced their mantras when they were living, will not need to wander very far down the bardo of dharmata. They will see the vidyadharas, the warriors, and the dakinis as soon as they stop breathing, and be invited into the Pure Realm of Space. There are many signs of this, including a clear sky, incense, music, and rays of light. Flowers will rain down from the sky, and they will dissolve into a rainbow of light.

Great teachers and philosophers, people who believe in tantra but have not continued with their samaya practice, and all other regular people require **The Great Liberation through Hearing**. People who meditate and who have practiced the Great Symbol and the Great Complete[49] will recognize the light of the bardo the moment before death, so they have no need to hear it.

If they recognize the bardo of the moment before death, they will reach the dharmakaya. If they recognize during the bardo of dharmata, when the peaceful and furious deities appear, they will reach Sambhogakaya. If they recognize during the bardo of becoming, they will reach Nirmanakaya. Here, they will be born into a better situation, and they will encounter **The Great Liberation through Hearing.** Because the results of actions continue into the next life, **The Great Liberation through Hearing** can enlighten even without meditation. People are liberated just because they hear it. Even great sinners are led along the secret path when they hear this teaching. In a single moment, ignorance is ended and enlightenment is instantly achieved. Sentient beings that have been reached by the teaching cannot possibly go into any lower existance.

**The Great Liberation through Hearing** and **The Liberation through Wearing** should be read out loud. Together, they are like a gold and turquoise mandala.

At this point, the importance of **The Great Liberation through Hearing** has been explained. Now, it is time to see how the bardo of the furious deities appears. One must call the name of the deceased three times and say the following:

"Oh noble child! Pay attention to what I am saying and don't allow yourself to be distracted. The bardo of the peaceful deities already appeared before you, but you did not recognize it, and have continued wandering. On the eighth day, a vision of the furious, blood-drinking deities will appear. Recognize them and pay attention.

"Oh noble child! The Glorious Great Buddha-Heruka[50] will come out of your mind, and you will see it clearly. His body is the color of wine. He has three heads, six arms, and four legs that are spread apart. His right face is white, his left face is red, and the one in the middle is the color of wine. His body burns like a bright light. He looks at you angrily with his nine eyes. His eyebrows are like lightning. His teeth shine like copper. He laughs loudly, shouting 'A-la-la' and 'Ha! ha!' He whistles loudly, 'Shoooo!'

"His hair is red and gold; it flies upwards and blazes. He wears crowns made of dried skulls, the sun, and the moon on his heads. His body is covered with black serpents and fresh skulls. He holds a wheel in the hand on the far right. The next hand holds an axe. The next hand holds a sword. He holds a bell in the hand on the far left. His next hand holds a plowshare. The next hand holds a skull-cup.

"His mate, Buddha-Krodhisvari, hugs his body. Her right hand is around his neck; her left hand holds a skull full of blood to his lips. He makes loud noises and roaring sounds. Flames of wisdom come out from every pore on his body. He stands on a throne that is supported by two garudas[51] . Two of his legs are bent and the other two are stretched out.

"Do not be scared. Do not be confused. Recognize that he is a form of your own mind. He is your yidam, so don't be afraid. Really he is the Blessed Vairocana with his mate, so don't be frightened. You will be liberated the moment you recognize."

When this is said, the deceased will recognize his yidam and merge with it. He will become a Buddha in the Sambhogakaya.

If the deceased is afraid, he will escape and will not recognize. In such a case, a vision of the blood-drinking Vajra family will appear. To show the deceased, one must call him by name and say these words:

"Oh noble child! Pay attention to what I am saying and don't allow yourself to be distracted. On the ninth day, a vision of the blood-drinking Vajra family will appear. This is the Blessed Vajra-Heruka. He will come from the eastern quarter of your mind. His body is dark blue. He has three heads, six arms, and four legs that are spread apart. His right face is white, his left face is red, and the one in the middle is the blue. He holds a vajra in the hand on the far right. His next hand holds a skull-cup. The next hand holds an axe. He holds a bell in the hand on the far left. His next hand holds a skull-cup. The next hand holds a plowshare.

"His mate, Vajra-Krodhisvari, hugs his body. Her right hand is around his neck; her left hand holds a skull full of blood to his lips.

"Do not be scared. Do not be confused. Recognize that he is a form of your own mind. He is your yidam, so don't be afraid. Really he is the Blessed Vajrasattva with his mate, so be devoted. You will be liberated the moment you recognize."

When this is said, the deceased will recognize his yidam and merge with it. He will become a Buddha in the Sambhogakaya.

If the deceased is has great karmic darkness, he will be afraid of it, escape, and not recognize it. In such a case, a vision of the blood-drinking Ratna family will appear on the tenth day. To show the deceased, one must call him by name and say these words:

"Oh noble child! Pay attention to what I am saying and don't allow yourself to be distracted. On the tenth day, a vision of the blood-drinking Ratna family will appear. This is the Blessed Ratna-Heruka. He will come from the southern quarter of your mind. His body is dark yellow. He has three heads, six arms, and four legs that are spread apart. His right face is white, his left face is red, and the one in the middle is a blazing dark yellow. He holds a jewel in the hand on the far right. His next hand holds a trident with three human heads. The next hand holds a club. He holds a bell in the hand on the far left. His next hand holds a skull-cup. The next hand holds a trident.

"His mate, Ratna-Krodhisvari, hugs his body. Her right hand is around his neck; her left hand holds a skull full of blood to his lips.

"Do not be scared. Do not be confused. Recognize that he is a form of your own mind. He is your yidam, so don't be afraid. Really he is the Blessed Ratnasambhava with his mate, so be devoted. You will be liberated the moment you recognize."

When this is said, the deceased will recognize his yidam and merge with it. He will become a Buddha.

If the deceased is pulled by unconscious and evil inclinations, he may be afraid and escape and not recognize his yidam. If he sees his Yamantaka and does not recognize him, then the blood-drinking vision of the Padma family will appear on the eleventh day. To show the deceased, one, must call him by name and say the following words:

"Oh noble child! Pay attention to what I am saying and don't allow yourself to be distracted. On the eleventh day, a vision of the blood-drinking Padma family will appear. This is the Blessed Padma-Heruka. He will come from the western quarter of your mind and appear clearly with his mate.

"His body is dark red. He has three heads, six arms, and four legs that are spread apart. His right face is white, his left face is red, and the one in the middle is a dark red.

He holds a lotus in the hand on the far right. His next hand holds a trident with three human heads. The next hand holds a rod. He holds a bell in the hand on the far left. His next hand holds a skull-cup. The next hand holds a small drum.

"His mate, Padma-Krodhisvari, hugs his body. Her right hand is around his neck; her left hand holds a skull full of blood to his lips.

"Do not be scared. Do not be confused. Be happy and recognize that he is a form of your own mind. He is your yidam, so don't be afraid. Really he is the Blessed Amitabha with his mate, so yearn for him. You will be liberated the moment you recognize."

When this is said, the deceased will recognize his yidam and merge with it. He will become a Buddha.

If the deceased is pulled by unconscious and evil inclinations, he may be afraid and escape and not recognize his yidam. In this case, the blood-drinking vision of the Karma family will appear on the twelfth day, with gauris[52], pisacis[53], and yoginis[54]. If he does not recognize them, he will be afraid, so to show the deceased, one must call him by name and say these words:

"Oh noble child! Pay attention to what I am saying and don't allow yourself to be distracted. On the twelfth day, a vision of the blood-drinking Karma family will appear. This is the Blessed Karma-Heruka. He will come from the northern quarter of your mind and appear clearly with his mate.

His body is dark green. He has three heads, six arms, and four legs that are spread apart. His right face is white, his left face is red, and the one in the middle is dark green. He holds a sword in the hand on the far right. His next hand holds a trident with three human heads. The next hand holds a rod. He holds a bell in the hand on the far left. His next hand holds a skull-cup. The next hand holds a plowshare.

“His mate, Karma-Krodhisvari, hugs his body. Her right hand is around his neck; her left hand holds a skull full of blood to his lips.

“Do not be scared. Do not be confused. Recognize that he is a form of your own mind. He is your yidam, so don’t be afraid. Really he is the Blessed Amoghasiddhi with his mate, so feel devoted to him. You will be liberated the moment you recognize.”

When this is said, the deceased will recognize his yidam and merge with it. He will become a Buddha.

The instruction of his guru will allow him to recognize these images as projections from his own mind, and he will be liberated. It is like seeing a stuffed lion. He will be very scared if he doesn’t know that it is just stuffed, but once someone shows him what it really is, he is surprised and no longer afraid.

In this case, too, the deceased will be scared and confused when he sees the blood-drinking deities, with their huge bodies and limbs. However, as soon as he recognizes that they are images that he has projected from his own mind, or as soon as he sees that they are yidams, the light upon which he used to meditate, and the self-existing light that comes later—the mother and the son—merge together. It is like meeting someone he knows very well. He spontaneously becomes liberated through the light of his own mind.

If the deceased does not receive this showing, even if he is a good person, he may turn back at this point. If he does this, he will wander again in samsara. In such a case, the eight angry gauris and the multi-headed pisacis will appear before him from his own mind. In such a case, one should call him by name and say these words:

"Oh noble child! Pay attention to what I am saying and don't allow yourself to be distracted. The eight gauris will appear to you as projections from your own mind. Don't be afraid.

The white Gauri will come from the eastern quarter of your mind. She holds a corpse like a club in her right hand, and a skull-cup filled with blood in her left hand. Don't be frightened. The yellow Cauri will come from the south shooting an arrow from a bow. The red Pramoha will come from the west, holding a banner of a sea-monster. The black Vetali will come frm the north, holding a vajra and a skull-cup with blood. The orange Pukkasi will come from the southeast holding intestines in her right hand and eating them with her left hand. The dark green Ghasmari will come from the southwest, holding a skull-cup in her left hand and drinking from it; stirring a vajra with her right hand. The pale yellow Candali will com from the northwest, tearing apart a head from a body, holding the heart in her right hand and eating the body with her left hand. The dark blue Smasani will come from the northeast, tearing apart a head from a body and eating.

"These eight gauris will surround the five blood-drinking herukas and will appear before you in your own mind. Do not be frightened.

"Oh noble child! Pay attention to what I am saying and don't allow yourself to be distracted. After these, the eight pisacis of the holy places will appear before you.

"The wine-colored, lion-headed Sinhamukha will come tossing her head from the east, with two hands crossed on her breast and a corpse in her mouth. The red, tiger-headed Vyaghrimukha will come from the south, with her arms crossed and pointing downwards, with her eyes staring and her teeth snarling. The black, fox-headed Srgalamukha will come from the west, holding a razor in her right hand and intestines in her left, eating them and licking up the blood. The dark blue wolf-headed Svanamukha will come from the north, carrying a corpse to her mouth with both hands, her eyes staring. The pale yellow vulture-headed Grdhraukha will come from the southeast, carrying a large dead body over her shoulder and holidng a skeleton in her hand. The dark red, hawk-headed Kankamukha will come from the southwest, carrying a large skin that has whip marks over her shoulder. The black, raven-headed Kakamukha will come from the northwest, with a skull-cup in her left hand and a sword in her right hand, and eating a heart and lungs. The dark blue owl-headed Ulumkha will come from the northeast, with a vajra in her right hand a sword in her lsft hand, eating.

"These eight pisacis of holy places will surround the five blood-drinking herukas and will appear before you in your own mind. Do not be frightened. Recognize what you see as an image that is being projected from your own mind.

"Oh noble child! The four goddesses of the gates will also appear before you in your mind. Recognize them.

The white tiger-headed Ankusa, from the eastern corner of your mind, will appear before you holding a goad[55] and a skull-cup filled with blood. The yellow, pig-headed Pasa, from the southern corner of your mind, will appear before you holding a noose. The red, lion-headed Srnkhala, from the west corner of your mind, will appear before you holding an iron chain. The green, serpent-headed Ghanta, from the north corner of your mind, will appear before you holding a bell.

"These four goddesses of the gates will come out of your mind and appear as images before you. Recognize them as yidams.

"Oh noble child! After the thirty angry herukas, the twenty-eight yoginis will appear from within your mind. You will see them with various heads and symbols. Don't be afraid. Recognize whatever you see as projections from your own mind. At this moment, remember the instructions you received from your guru.

"Oh noble child! The six yoginis from the east will come out from your mind and appear before you, as follows: The wine-colored yak-headed demon Raksasi with a vajra in her hand. The orange, serpent-headed Brahmi with a lotus in her hand. The dark green leopard-headed Mahadevi, the Great Goddess, with a trident in her hand. The blue mongoose-headed Lobha, the greedy one, with a wheel in her hand. The red Kumari, with her yellow bear head, holding a short spear in her hand. The white Indrani, with her brown bear head, holding a noose of intestines in her hand.

"Do not be afraid of them.

"Oh noble child! The six yoginis from the south will come out from your mind and appear before you, as follows: The yellow pig-headed Vajra with a razor in her hand. The red Santi, Peace, with her sea-monster head, holding a vase in her hand. The red scorpion-headed Amrta, Nectar of Immortality, with the lotus in her hand. The white hawk-headed Danda, Moon, with a vajra in her hand. The dark green fox-headed Danda, Club, with a club in her hand. The dark yellow tiger-headed Raksasi, the Demon, holding a skull full of blood in her hand. The white Indrani, with her brown bear head, holding a noose of intestines in her hand.

"Do not be afraid of them.

"Oh noble child! The six yoginis from the west will come out from your mind and appear before you, as follows:

The dark green vulture-headed Bhaksini, Eater, with a club in her hand. The red horse-headed Rati, Pleasure, with a large trunk from a corpse in her hand. The white garuda-headed Mahabala, Great Strength, with a club in her hand. The red dog-headed Raksasi, Demon, cutting with a vajra-razor in her hand. The red Kama, Desire, with the head of a poopoe, shooting an arrow from a bow in her hand. The dark green deer-headed Vasuraksa, Protector of Wealth, with a vase in her hand.

"Do not be afraid of them.

"Oh noble child! The six yoginis from the north will come out from your mind and appear before you, as follows: The blue wolf-headed Vayudevi, Wind-Goddess, waving a flag in her hand. The red buffalo-headed Nari, Woman, holding a stake in her hand. The black, pig-headed Varahi, holding a noose of teeth. The red, crow-headed Vajra, holding the skin of a child in her hand. The dark green elephant-headed Mahahastini, Elephant, holidng a large corpse in her hand and drinking its blood. The blue, serpent-headed Varunadevi, Water-Goddess, holidng a noose of snakes.

"Do not be afraid of them.

"Oh noble child! The four yoginis of the gates will come out of your mind and appear before you, as follows: From the east, the white, cuckoo-headed Vajra, holding an iron hook. From the south, the yellow goat-headed Vajra, holding a nose. From the west, the red, lion-headed Vajra, with an iron chain in her hand. From the north, the dark green serpent-headed Vajra, with a bell in her hand. These four yoginis of the gates will come out from your mind and appear before you.

"These twenty-eight yoginis will come into your mind spontaneously, from the play of existing wrathful herukas. Recognize them.

"Oh noble child! From out of the emptiness, the dharmakaya appears as the peaceful deities. Recognize it. If you know that these fifty-eight blood-drinking deities appeared to you from your mind, appeared from your own radiant insight, then you will immediately become a Buddha, and merge with these blood-drinking deities.

"Oh noble child! If you do not recognize that this is how it is, you will be frightened and escape. If you do this, you will suffer more.

"If you do not recognize now, you will see all the blood-drinking deities as Lords of Death. You will be frightened and scared. You will be confused and weak. Your thoughts will become your demons and you will wander in samsara. But, if you are neither drawn to them nor afraid, you will not wander in samsara.

"Oh noble child! These peaceful and furious deities are immense. The largest is as big as the whole sky. The medium-sized ones are as big as Mount Meru[56]. The smallest ones are as tall as eighteen people stacked on top of each other. Do not be frightened. These phenomena appear as lights and visions. If you recognize these appearances as the natural light of your own mind, you will merge with these lights and images, and become a Buddha.

"Oh noble child! No matter how terrifying the vision you see is, recognize that it is a projection of your own mind. If you can do this, you will instantly become a Buddha. It is clear. Perfect, immediate enlightenment will occur immediately. Remember!

"Oh noble child! If you are still scared, and if you don't recognize now, all the peaceful deities will appear as Mahakala. All of the furious deities will appear as the Dharma King, as the Lord of Death.

The images you project from your mind will turn into demons, and you will wander in samsara.

"Oh noble child! Even if you have practiced meditating for years and years, even if you know all the sutras and tantras, if you do not recognize your own projections now, you will not become a Buddha. If you do recognize them, however, you will become a Buddha with a single word and a single secret.

"If you don't recognize the images you are projecting, they will appear in the form of the Dharma King, the Lord of Death, in the bardo of dharmata as soon as you are dead. The largest bodies of the Lord of Death are as big as the whole sky. The medium-sized ones are as big as Mount Meru. They will fill the whole universe. Their teeth bite their lower lips and their eyes are glassy. Their hair is tied at the tops of their heads, and they have huge bellies and skinny necks. They hold the records of karma in their hands and shout 'Strike!' and 'Kill!' They lick up brains, tear heads from bodies, and pull out people's internal organs. This is how they appear, and they fill the whole universe.

"Oh noble child! Don't be afraid by these projections. Your mind is full of unconscious inclinations. Even if you are killed and chopped up, you will not die. You are emptiness in its natural form. You have nothing to fear.

“The Lords of Death come from your mind also. They have no physicality, they are totally intangible. Emptiness can’t be hurt by emptiness. Know that these deities—the external peaceful and furious deities, the blood-drinking herukas, the animal-headed deities, the rainbow light, the Lords of Death—they are all intangible. They come from your mind. If you can understand this, then your fear will be set free, and you will merge inseparably to become a Buddha. These are your yidams, if you can recognize them.

“With intense desire, think to yourself, ‘They are here to guide me along the dangerous path of the bardo. I will find safety in them. Remember the Three Jewels. Remember your yidam. Call your yidam by name and plead with it by saying the following: ‘I am wandering in the bardo. Please, rescue me. Grab me with your compassion, dear yidam.’ Call your guru by name and plead with him by saying: ‘I am wandering in the bardo. Please, rescue me. Be compassionate and don’t abandon me.’ Plead achingly with the blood-drinking deities and say this inspirational prayer:

When I wander in samsara,
Due to my strong unconscious
  inclinations,
In the shining light of being fearless,
May the peaceful and furious Blessed
Ones lead me,
And may the angry goddesses, the
Queens of Space,
Come behind me.
May they help me to cross,
The bardo's dangerous path,
And bring me to the perfect Buddha
  state.

When I am alone, away from my dear
  friends,
When the empty images from my own
  thoughts appear,
May the Buddhas send out the power
  from their compassion,
So that the terrors of the bardo do not
  come.
May I recognize myself,
When the bright lights of wisdom shine.
May I recognize the bardo,
When the images of the peaceful and
  furious deities appear.
May my yidam remove all pain,

When I suffer from evil karma.
When dharmata roars with the sound of
a thousand thunders,
May it all sound like just six syllables.
When I have no shelter,
And when I follow my karma,
May the Lord of Great Compassion be a
shelter for me.
May the samadhi of happiness and light
come when I suffer from the karma of
unconscious inclinations.
May the five elements not be enemies.
May I see the region of the five
Buddhas.

"It is very important that you are not distracted as you say this inspirational prayer. You must say it with all your heart. If you do, your fears will disappear, and you will become a Buddha in the Sambhogakaya."

Repeat these words three times, or up to seven times. Regardless of sins, and regardless of how much bad karma remains, it is impossible not be liberated. However, if the deceased still does not recognize, he must continue wandering. Now he will wander into the third bardo, the bardo of becoming. The manner in which it appears is described below:

Most people are confused by fear during the bardo of the moment of death. This happens to people who did not meditate a lot during their life, as well as people who did. These people can only be liberated through **The Great Liberation through Hearing**. For people who have meditated a lot, however, the bardo of dharmata comes quite suddenly when their mind and body are separated. People who were able to see their own mind while they lived are very strong when the light of the moment before death appears. For this reason, meditating during life is important. People who meditated on the generation and perfection stages of the tantric deities while they were living are particularly strong when the images of peaceful and furious deities appear during the bardo of dharmata. For these reasons, it is very important to learn **The Liberation through Hearing in the Bardo** while one is alive, and to train the mind accordingly.

**The Liberation through Hearing in the Bardo** should be understood during life. It should be read out loud and memorized. It should be practiced three times every day. Its meaning should be completely clear. Its words and meanings should never be forgotten, even if one is chased by a hundred murderers. This is **The Great Liberation through Hearing**, so even people who have committed the five deadly sins can be liberated just by hearing it. Therefore, it should be read aloud all over, among diverse people, and to great crowds.

Even if a person has heard it only once, and even then didn't understand its meaning, it can be remembered perfectly—without a single word forgotten—during the bardo state, because the mind is nine times clearer than it is usually. For this reason, everyone should hear it during their lifetime. It should be read beside people who are sick and people who are dying. It should be read all over the world.

It is truly good luck to hear these teachings. Indeed, unless a person deserves it, unless someone has cleared away the darkness from their minds, it is hard to hear. If one hears it, one becomes liberated just by not disbelieving. For these reasons, cherish this doctrine. It brings out the essence of all dharma.

This is the end of the exposure of the bardo of dharmata, **The Great Liberation through Hearing**. It is the bardo teaching that has the ability to liberate simply by being heard and seen.

With reverence to the deities, the gurus,
the yidams, and the dakinis.
May they bring about liberation in the
bardo.
The bardo of dharmata was taught,
in the above, through **The Great Liberation through Hearing**
Now is the reminder of the bardo of
becoming.

The bardo of dharmata has already been shown many times. For people who are good at meditating on karma, or for people who have good karma, it might be enough for recognition. However, for people who are not good at meditating, and for people who were very evil in their lives, recognizing it may have been difficult due to fear and bad karma. So, starting on the tenth day, these words should be spoken, as a reminder:

"Oh noble child! Listen closely and understand. Creatures who are born in hell, or in the world of devas, or in the body of the bardo, are all born spontaneously, and experience a supernatural birth. You were frightened by the peaceful and furious deities that appeared in the bardo of dharmata. You didn't recognize them and you fainted after five and a half days. When you recovered, your mind was clear, and a body like your own body, your previous body, arose. The tantra says:

> In the bardo of becoming,
> The former and the future body wander freely,
> With all of their senses.
> Due to karma, they possess the power of miracles,
> Seen by the eyes of deities,
> That are similar in nature.

"In this passage, 'former' means that the body you have now is like the body you had in the past, made of flesh and blood, because you remember that body. However, this body is different, because it glows, and has marks like the bodies of those will higher destinies.

"This body is created by the mind, so it is called a mental body of the bardo experience. At this moment, if you are going to be born as a deva, you will experience the realm of the devas. That is, if you are going to be born as a jealous deity, a human being, an animal, a hungry ghost or a creature from hell, you will have this experience at this moment.

For four and a half days you will think about your former body, the one that had memories of your former self. Future refers to the experiences you will have after you are born again. That is the meaning of future and former.

"Don't be drawn to any images at this time. Do not desire them either. If you are drawn or desire images, you will wander in the six realms and be miserable.

"The images of the bardo of dharmata appeared until yesterday, but you didn't recognize them. Because of this, you have to wander here. If you can meditate without distraction now, if you can relax in a pure, illuminated, and empty mind, just as your guru showed you, if you can rest without understanding and without action, you will be liberated, and will not enter a womb.

"If you cannot recognize, imagine your yidam or your guru above you. Strongly feel a great sense devotion. This is crucial, so you must not let yourself be distracted."

One should say these words. If one recognizes now, one will be freed, and will not wander in the six realms. However, if one is being influenced by bad karma, one will have difficulty recognizing. In that case, the following must be said:

"Oh noble child! Pay attention to what I am saying and don't allow yourself to be distracted. The phrase 'complete in all senses' means that even if you were blind, deaf, or lame when you were alive, you will see, hear and be fully able in the bardo state. All of your senses will function clearly and perfectly. That is what it means to be "complete in all the sense." This is a sign that you have died, and that you are wandering in a bardo state. So recognize this situation and remember your instructions.

"Oh noble child! The phrase 'without obstruction' means your body and mind are separate. You have no physical body; only a mental body. This means you can move through Mount Meru, the king of mountains, or anywhere else you like, except for your mother's womb, and the vajra seat[57]. This is a sign that you are wandering the in the bardo of becoming, so remember your guru's instructions and pray to the Lord of Great Compassion.

"Oh noble child! The phrase 'having miraculous powers due to karma' means that you have great powers now, due to the power of the karma according to you actions, powers beyond those that come from meditation or good qualities. In a single instant, you can travel through the four continents and Mount Meru. You can go anywhere you want as soon as you think about it, or in the amount of time it takes for a person to stretch out his hand and draw it back again. These powers, however, are not appropriate. Do not think about them. You can show them now without any problem, you can do anything you want to do—there is nothing you cannot do! So recognize this, and pray to your guru.

"Oh noble child! The phrase 'seen by the pure eyes of similar deities' means those who will be reborn with the same nature will see each other in this bardo state. Those who will be born as deities will see each other too. So, regardless of the realm they will be born into, those that will be born into the same realm will see each other. Do not long for them, but concentrate on the Lord of Great Compassion. The phrase 'seen by the pure eyes of deities' also means seen by the pure eyes of those meditating in the real samadhi. It does not only mean that which is earned from the deities because the deities do not always see. If they concentrate on seeing they will see, but if they don't see, or if their thoughts are disturbed, they will not see.

"Oh noble child! In this type of body, you will see

your home and your family. You will feel as if you are meeting them in a dream. You may even speak to them, but they will not answer you. You will see your family crying and you'll think to yourself, 'I am dead. What can I do?'

"You will feel pain, great pain. You will feel pain as a fish feels pain when it is rolling in hot sand, rather than swimming in water. Suffering, however, is no use now. If you have a guru, plead with him. Or plead with the yidam, the Lord of Great Compassion.

"You may feel attached to your relatives, but this is useless, so let yourself go. There will be no suffering or fear if you plead with the Lord of Great Compassion.

"Oh noble child! You are blown by the wind of karma. Your mind has no support. You are riding the wind helplessly. You are like a feather that is being blown this way and that way.

"You will say to the mourners, 'I am here! Don't cry!' But they will not notice you. You'll think to yourself, 'I have died, and you'll feel great pain. Don't suffer. There will be a gray haze—like the grey of dawn in autumn—a gray that is neither night nor day. This type of bardo state may last for one or two weeks—it may even last for six or seven weeks. People say suffering in the bardo of becoming lasts for three weeks, but this is not definite, because karma effects the amount of time.

"Oh noble child! The great tornado of karma will come from behind you at this moment. It is terrifying and unbearable; it whirls around you fiercely. Don't be frightened. It is a confused image from your own mind. In front of you it will be dark and dense. It is terrifying and awful and there are terrible shouts of 'Strike!' and 'Kill!' Do not be afraid of these sounds. For others, for people who have done great evil in their lives, their karma will cause flesh-eating demons to appear. These demons will carry all types of terrible weapons. They will shout out cries of battle. They will shout things like 'Strike! and 'Kill!'

"You will feel as if you are being chased by terrifying beasts. You will feel as if a huge army of snow, rain, storms and darkness is following you. You will hear the sounds of mountains falling to the ground, of lakes flooding over, of fire spreading, and of terrible winds blowing. You will try to escape—in any possible direction—but you will be faced by three sharp and terrifying cliffs. The cliffs are red, white and black. You will almost fall over them.

“Oh noble child! They are not really cliffs. They are aggression, passion and ignorance. Recognize that this is the bardo of becoming and call to the Lord of Great Compassion, as follow: ‘Oh Lord of Great Compassion, my guru, the Three Jewels, do not let me, [INSERT NAME], fall into hell.’ Plead with passion. Do not forget.

“As for others, for people who have behaved properly, people who have practiced dharma in earnest, they will be invited by all sorts of wonderful pleasures. They will experience perfect happiness and joy. As for people who were ignorant or did not care, who didn’t do good, but didn’t do evil either, they will experience neither pleasure nor pain. Instead, they will see ignorance and indifference.

“Oh noble child! Whatever happens in this situation, whatever desirable items appear, do not let yourself be drawn to them. Do not want them. Offer them to your guru, and the Three Jewels. Do not allow your heart to feel desire. And if you feel indifference, if this occurs without feelings of pleasure or pain, allow your mind to rest, in the Great Symbol state of concentration, without meditation. This is very important.

“Oh noble child! You will be sheltered for

the moment by places such as bridges, shrines, monasteries, huts, and stupas[58], but do not stay here for long. Your mind and body are separated, so you cannot relax or settle. You feel angry and cold. Your consciousness is not stable. It moves quickly and becomes airy. You think to yourself, 'Oh! I am dead! What can I do now?' With this thought, your heart will become cold. You feel empty. You will feel intense, endless, terrible pain. You must move on—you cannot settle in a single place—so don't let your mind become occupied with thoughts. Allow your mind to rest, in its fundamental state.

"At a certain time, you will have no food other than that which has been dedicated for you by your family. There is also no guarantee that you will have any friends. These are signs that your mind is wandering in the bardo of becoming. At this moment, your karma will determine what hurts and what is pleasant. You will see your home, your friends, your family. You will see your own dead body. You will think, 'I am dead, now. What can I do?' Your mind will suffer a lot. You will think to yourself, 'Maybe I should find a body.' You will start searching all over for a body.

"You may be able to enter your own dead body as many as nine times, but you will find it cold, as if frozen by winter. You will find it putrid, as if rotted by the heat of the summer. Maybe your family will have burned it or maybe it has been buried or maybe it was eaten by birds and wild animals. It has been a long time since you entered the bardo of dharmata, and you will find no way of entering your body. You will feel great despair. You will feel as though you are being squeezed between rocks and stones. This feeling—this suffering—is part of the bardo of becoming. Even if you look for a body you will only find suffering, so stop wanting a body and relax and concentrate in this state of non-action."

One can be liberated in this bardo if shown in this way. However, if one cannot be shown and if one cannot recognize because of bad karma, the dead person's name should be called, and these words should be said.

"Oh noble child [INSERT NAME]! Listen! You are suffering like this because of your own karma, so don't blame anyone else. Plead passionately with the Three Jewels and they will protect you. If you don't plead, if you don't know the Great Symbol meditation and don't meditate on your own yidam, then your good conscience will count your good deeds as white pebbles, and your own bad conscience will count your bad deeds as black pebbles. You will be terrified at this moment. You will shake and tremble. You will lie and say you have not sinned. In this situation, the Lord of Death will say: 'I will look in the mirror of your karma.' All of your bad and good deeds will appear in this mirror—clearly and accurately—and your lie will be useless. The Lord of Death will tie a rope around your neck and drag you. He will cut off your head. He will tear out your heart. He will pull out your intestines and eat your brains and drink your blood and eat your flesh and chew on your bones. You, however, cannot die. And so even though your body has been destroyed, you will recover.

"It hurts a lot being cut up into pieces, so don't be frightened when the white pebbles are counted. Don't fear the Lord of Death and don't tell lies. You only exist mentally, and so you can't die, even if you are killed and cut into pieces. You are the most natural form of emptiness, so don't be afraid.

"The Lords of Death are emptiness in its natural form. They are images you have created, projecting them in your confused mind. You are emptiness. You are a mental body that is behaving unconsciously. Emptiness cannot be harmed by emptiness. Things that have no shape and no character cannot harm other things that do not have shape or character.

Beings such as the Lords of Death, the deities, the evil spirits, the Bull-headed demon, etc., only exist in the images you project in your mind. Recognize this, and everything else, at this moment as the bardo.

"Think about the samadhi of the Great Symbol. If you don't know how to meditate, then think about what sorts of things frighten you. You will see that emptiness has no nature whatsoever. This is the dharmakaya. This emptiness is not nothingness. The nature of it is frightening; it awes the mind with its clarity. This is the state of mind of the Sambhogakaya.

"Emptiness and brightness are not two separate things. The nature of emptiness is brightness and the nature of brightness is emptiness. The two are inseparable. The mind is now naked in this uncreated state. It is both empty and bright. This is svabhavikakaya. Its natural energy arises everywhere. It is not blocked. It is the compassionate Nirmanakaya.

"Oh noble child! See this and don't be distracted. As soon as you recognize, you will be enlightened in all four kayas. Don't be distracted. This is the point at which Buddhas and sentient beings are separated.

If you do not pay attention now, it will be ages before you come out of this misery.

"There is a saying about this moment. It is:

They are separated in a moment,
Perfect enlightenment occurs in a moment.

"You were distracted until yesterday. Even though so much of the bardo state has appeared, you were so frightened that you did not recognize it. If you are still distracted now, the rope of compassion will be cut. You will have to go to a place where there is no liberation. So be careful!"

Even someone who has not recognized before will recognize now, and will be liberated. If the person is untrained, if he doesn't know how to meditate, one should say the following:

"Oh noble child! If you don't know how to meditate, then remember the Buddha and the Dharma. Remember the Sangha and the Lord of Great Compassion. Plead with them. Think about all of these terrifying images as your own yidam, or as the Lord of Great Compassion, and plead with them. Remember your guru, and the mystic name you had in the world of humans, and tell it to the Dharma

King, to the Lord of Death. Don't be frightened. Don't be scared. Even if you fall down the cliff, you will not be hurt."

After being shown these words, the deceased will be liberated now, even if he wasn't before. However, there is still a possibility that he won't be liberated, so it is important to try again. It is important to call the deceased by name and to say these words:

"What you are experiencing now will make you happy, then sad, then happy again. Every moment, you will alternate between these feelings, as though you are on a catapult. So don't feel any passion or violent anger.

"If you are going to be born on a higher level, you may be having visions of that level while your relatives are making animal sacrifices for the sake of the dead. Bad thoughts may come to your mind, causing you to feel anger. If this happens, you will be born as a creature of hell. So, regardless of what is happening in the place you have left behind, don't be angry. Only think about love and kindness.

"If you feel connected to possessions you used to have, if you feel connected to them simply because someone else now owns them and is enjoying them, you will be angry. If you are angry with the people you left behind, you will definitely be born in hell, or you will become a hungry ghost, even if you were supposed to reach a higher level. No matter what, you cannot have the things you left behind. It's a useless feeling, so just give up your possessions—and your desire for your possessions. Make a conscious decision to give them up. It doesn't matter who is using your possessions. Just give them up. Accept that they are not yours. Concentrate deeply on offering these possessions to your guru and the Three Jewels, and stay in a state without desire.

"When the konkani mantra for the dead is on your behalf, or when the ritual for purifying from lower levels is conducted for you, you will be able to see them being conducted with discreet, supernatural abilities. You will see that they are being done impurely or sleepily; you will see that people are not attentive, or they are not behaving carefully and are not obeying the samaya vows. You will sense their lack of faith, the sense that they don't believe. You will sense things are done out of fear, bad activities, or impurities in the rituals. You will think to yourself, 'Oh! They must be playing a trick on me. They are trying to deceive me.' These thoughts will cause you great sadness and despair. On top of everything, you will not feel devoted. You will not believe. You will lose your faith. This will cause to sink into even lower planes.

"These thoughts are useless and will cause you great harm. So, regardless of whether the rituals performed by the spiritual friends you have left behind are impure or not, let your own thoughts be pure, full of faith, and devotion. Think to yourself, 'Well! The images I am projecting must be impure! How is it possible for there to be impurity in Buddha's words? These must be a result of my own impure thoughts, like seeing my reflection and noticing the faults on my face. As for these people, their body is the sangha[59], their speech is the dharma, their mind is the nature of Buddha. So, I must find shelter in them.' By thinking these thoughts, everything that happens in the place you left will help you, so it is very important to have pure thoughts like these. Don't forget.

"It is very helpful, especially if you were going to be born into one of the three lower planes. If this is the case, and if you look at the rituals that your relatives are performing in the place you left and perceive them to be pure and free of sin, then you will feel great joy. If you see that the gurus and teachers are practicing dharma with total purity, in their bodies, their words and their thoughts, you will feel great joy. This will cause you to be born in a higher realm, right away! For this reason, it is very important to have pure thoughts, and to feel devotion without prejudice.

"Oh noble child! Let me sum everything up. Your mind is in the bardo state, now. It has no support, no firm object to depend upon. It is light and free to move. Whatever thoughts you have now, whether they are good or bad, are very powerful. Do not think of bad things; think only of good things. If you don't have any experience in the practice, then just feel dedication and pure thoughts. Plead with your yidam, and with the Lord of Great Compassion, and say this inspirational prayer with great concentration:

When wandering alone,
Away from dear friends,
The empty forms of the images I am
  projecting appear.
May the Buddhas send out the power of
  their compassion,
So that the terrors of the bardo don't
  come.
When I suffer from evil karma,
May my yidam get rid of the misery.
When I hear the roar of the dharmata,
Which sounds like a thousand thunders,

May it sound like six syllables.
When I follow my karma, without any shelter,
May the Lord of Great Compassion protect me.
When I suffer because of the karma of unconscious inclinations,
May the happiness and light of samadhi come."

If you say this prayer passionately, there is no doubt that it will lead you on the path. It is very important that you believe in this prayer as you say it."

When this prayer is said, the deceased will remember, recognize, and become liberated. However, even if one repeats this many times, it may be difficult to recognize because of the effect of bad karma. In this case, it is very helpful to repeat the prayer over and over again. One should call the deceased by name and say the following words:

"Oh noble child! If you haven't understood what has happened until now, the body in your past life will now become dimmer. The body in your future life will become more real. You may feel sad by this. You may think, 'I am suffering so much now. I am miserable. I will take whatever body I can find, whatever body appears.' With this thought, you will wander all over the place, backwards and forwards, endlessly and in confusion. At this time, six lights, from the six planes of existence, will shine. The light from the plane where you are going to be born again will shine the most brightly.

"Oh noble child! Listen. If you ask what these lights are, here is the answer. From the devas comes the dim white light, and from the jealous deities comes the red light. The blue light comes from human beings and the green light comes from animals. From the hungry ghosts comes the yellow light, and from the creatures of hell comes the smoke-colored light. These are the six lights. At that moment, your body will take on the color of the light from the place where you are to be born.

"Oh noble child! The main point of the teachings is very important now. Whatever light shines, that is light you must meditate upon, as the Lord of the Great Compassion. Think deeply that when the light appears, it is the Lord of Great Compassion. This is the most important thought. It is crucial, as it is the thought that prevents birth.

"Meditate on your yidam for a long time. Think about it as a vision, as an entity that does not have any real essence on its own. It is a purely imagined being. Then, let the yidam dissolve, starting at the edges and working toward the center. Rest for a while in the state of emptiness and brightness, this inconceivable state which actually consists of nothing at all.

"Think about the yidam again, then think about the brightness. Continue to meditate in this manner, and then let your mind dissolve inward from the edges, also. Wherever there is emptiness, there is mind; wherever there is mind, there is dharmakaya. Relax in this simple and selfless state of dharmakaya."

"Birth cannot happen in this state, and the deceased will achieve perfect enlightenment. However, those who were not devoted to practice, and those who are not skilled at meditation will not understand. They will continue to wander, confused, towards the womb. For this reason, instructions for closing the womb are very important. One should call the deceased by name and say the following:

"Oh noble child! If you didn't recognize what was happening until now, you will now feel that you are moving. The force of karma will move you upwards or downwards or sideways. At this moment, think about the Lord of Great Compassion. Remember!

“Then, as was said before, you will feel wind, snow, and hail. You will feel as if people are chasing you and you are trying to escape. People who do not have good qualities will feel as though they are running away to miserable places. Those that have some good karma will feel as if they are arriving at a place of joy and happiness.

“At this moment, oh noble child, signs of the place where you were born will appear before you. Listen closely. Don’t let yourself be distracted. There are many important instructions that must follow. Even though you did not understand how to recognize until now, even someone who is very weak in his practice will be able to recognize now. Listen closely!

“It is very important to carefully close the door of the womb at this moment. There are two ways of doing this. One way is by stopping the person who is entering the womb. The other way is by closing up the womb entrance. Here are instructions for stopping the person who is about to enter the womb:

“Oh noble child [INSERT NAME]! Think about your yidam. Create an image in your mind, one that has no real substance, an illusion, much like the image of the moon reflected on water. If you don’t have a specific yidam, then imagine the Lord of Great Compassion. Imagine him vividly. Then, let the yidam dissolve, from the edges and towards the center. Think about the brightness-emptiness blankly. This is the deep secret. It is said that in this manner, one can avoid entering the womb, so think in this way.

"But if this is not enough to stop you from entering the womb, and if you are about to enter it anyway, there are insightful instructions for how to close the womb entrance. Listen to these instructions. Repeat after me. These words are from the main verses of the bardo.

> Now, when the bardo of becoming is
>   dawning on me,
> I will concentrate deeply and try to hold
>   on to good karma,
> To close the entrance to the womb, and
>   to think of resistance.
> This is the moment when determination
>   is necessary,
> When pure thought is critical,
> When jealousy must be abandoned,
> And when meditation upon the guru and
>   his mate is necessary.

Clearly say these words, with your own voice.

Clearly remember their meaning. Meditate on these words and implement them.

"This is the meaning of the words: 'Now, when the bardo of becoming is dawning on me,' means now that you are wandering in the bardo of becoming. To see signs of this, look in the water. You will not see your reflection. You can also notice that your body has no shadow. You don't have any physical body. You also don't have any flesh or blood. These are signs that the mental body is wandering in the bardo of becoming.

"At this time, you must concentrate deeply and without distraction. At this moment, total concentration is the most important thing. It is like controlling a horse by its reins. Whatever you think about will happen, so don't think about anything that is bad. Remember the dharma and remember your teachings. Think about the spiritual relationships, and about the people who read to you religious texts such as **The Great Liberation through Hearing** while you were in the human world. Work hard to extend the results of good karma. It is very important. Don't forget and don't allow yourself to be distracted. Now is the dividing time, the time that is the boundary. You may go up and you may go down. If you become lazy now—even for a moment—you will suffer forever. However, if you concentrate with all your mind, you will be happy forever. Concentrate deeply and strive to continue in this series of good karma.

"Now is the time to close the entrance to the womb:

> Close the entrance of the womb,
> And think about resisting.
> This is the time when one must persevere,
> And think pure thoughts.

Now is the time. First, the entrance to the womb must be closed. There are five ways of doing this, so be sure you understand them well.

"Oh noble child! You will see images of males and females having sex at this time. When you see them, hold yourself back, and do not come between them. Remember and think they are the guru and his mate. In your mind, bow down to them. Make offerings to them with great and wholehearted devotion. Ask them for religious guidance. When you concentrate deeply on this thought, the entrance to the womb will definitely close.

"However, if the entrance to the womb does not

close, and if you are about to enter it, think about the guru and his mate as though they are your yidam, or the Lord of Great Compassion with his consort, and make them an offering in your mind. Ask them to give you spiritual benefits. Ask them with great devotion, and this will close the entrance to the womb.

"However, if the entrance to the womb does not close, and if you are about to enter it, here is a third way for repelling desire and violent anger. There are four types of birth: birth from an egg; birth from a womb, spontaneous, supernatural birth, and birth from moisture. Of these births, birth from an egg and from a womb are quite similar. As described above, there will be images of males and females having sex. If you enter the womb at this moment, through powerful feelings of desire and disgust, you may be born as a horse, a bird, a dog, a human, etc. If you are going to be born masculine, you will have feelings of being male. You will feel violent and intense hatred toward the father. You will feel jealousy toward the father, and be attracted to the mother. If you are going to be born feminine, you will have feelings of being female. You will feel violence and intense hatred toward the mother. You will feel jealousy toward the mother, and be attracted to the father. This will cause you to enter the path that leads to the womb. You will feel great happiness as the sperm and egg meet. In that deeply happy state, you will become unconscious. The embryo will grow; it will become round and oblong. It will continue to grow until it comes out of the mother's womb. You will open your eyes and you will be a puppy. First you were a man and now you are a dog, so you will suffer in a doghouse. Or you will open your eyes and find yourself as a pig, living in a pigsty. Or you will be an ant and live in an anthill. Or you will be a worm that lives in a hole in the ground. Or you will be a calf or a goat or a lamb. From this situation, there is no return. You will have to suffer all kinds of suffering. You will be in a state of great stupidity and ignorance. In this manner, one may wander through the six states of existence, of creatures from hell, of hungry ghosts, etc. You will live through endless suffering. This is the most powerful and terrible thing. Terrible! Terrible! Those who have not been instructed by a guru will fall off the cliff of samsara in this manner. They will suffer endlessly and unbearably. So, rather than suffering this fate, listen to what I say, and understand my instructions.

"The instructions for rejecting feelings of desire and disgust are as follows. Listen to these instructions and understand them in order to close the entrance to the womb. It is said:

Close the entrance to the womb,
Think of resistance.
This is the time when one must be
  dedicated,
And when pure thoughts are necessary.
Leave jealousy aside, and meditate on
  the guru and his mate.

As explained earlier, you will feel jealousy. If you are going to be born masculine, you will be attracted to the mother and despise the father. If you are going to be born female, you will be attracted to the father and despise the mother. There is an intense teaching for this time.

"Oh noble child! When there are feelings of attraction and violent anger such as these, meditate in the following manner: 'Alas! I have such evil karma that I have been wandering in samsara until now, because I have not let go of my feelings of desire and violent anger. If I continue to feel this way, I will wander in samsara forever. I will sink into an ocean of suffering for a very long time. So now I don't feel any desire or disgust at all. Alas! Now I will never feel desire or disgust again.' If you concentrate deeply on this thought, the tantras say that this is enough to close the entrance to the womb. Oh noble child! Don't let yourself be distracted. Concentrate fully with your mind.

"However, maybe the entrance to the womb will not be closed by this. Maybe you are still about to enter the womb. In such a case, it should be closed by teachings about how the nature of everything is unreal and false. Meditate in this manner: 'Alas! The father and the mother, the dark rain and the strong wing, the thunder and the frightening images, and all of these phenomena are false in their real nature. Regardless of how they seem, they are not real. All items of substance are fake and unreal. They are like a dream, an image. They are not permanent, they are not always the same. What purpose is there in desire? What purpose is there in fear? With these emotions, one simply perceives the non-existent as though they exist. These are all images from my mind, and since the mind is illusory to begin with, since the mind does not actually exist from the very beginning, where can these things arise from externally? In the past, I didn't have this understanding. I believed that the nonexistent existed, that the false was true, that illusions were real. Because of this, I have wandered in samsara for such a long time. Furthermore, if I don't realize that they are illusions now, I will continue to wander in samsara for a long time, and I will definitely become mired in misery. Now they are all dreams. They are all like illusions, like echoes, like the cities of gandharvas[60]. They are all mirages, images, optical illusions. They are like the moon reflected in the water. They are not real, not at all, not even for a moment. The truth is they are false!'

"With this single-minded train of thought, one can destroy any belief in the reality of these things, and when one has convinced oneself in this manner, belief in a self is neutralized. In you truly understand unreality in this way, if you understand this from the depth of your heart, then the entrance to the womb will definitely be closed.

"However, even after doing this, if the belief in reality is not destroyed, the entrance to the womb will not be closed. You will be about to enter the womb, and to stop this, there is another meaningful teaching.

"Oh noble child! If the entrance to the womb has not been closed yet, the fifth method, the meditation on light, should be able to close it. This meditation is done in the following manner: 'All substances are my own mind, and this mind is empty, unborn, unblocked.' Continue to think these thoughts and allow your mind to rest in its natural, unformed state, a state that is contained by its own nature, like water that is poured into water. If the mind is allowed to rest naturally, freely, then the entrance to the womb for all kinds of birth will most certainly be closed."

Many true and meaningful instructions on how to close the entrance to the womb have just been described. Anyone who has high, average or even low abilities will be liberated by these instructions. It is not possible for it to be otherwise. Why is this? The first reason is that consciousness in the bardo state includes a supernatural ability to perceive worldly things. So, the deceased can hear what is said. The second reason is that even if a person was deaf, blind and lame in life, all of their senses now function perfectly, so the person can hear what is being said. The third reason is that the deceased is so totally frightened that he is concentrating completely on what he can do. Therefore, he listens to what I am saying. The fourth reason is that the conscious has no support—it goes wherever it is guided by concentration—and so it is easy to guide. At this time, the mind is nine times clearer than it was before, so even if the deceased person was not smart, the karma of the mind is very forceful, and becomes so clear that it can meditate on whatever is taught. These essential points are the reason. It is also helpful to perform the rituals for the dead, and for the same reasons.

For these reasons, it is very important to continue reading **The Great Liberation through Hearing** for up to forty-nine days. Although the deceased may not be liberated at one exposure, he will be liberated at another. For this reason, many exposures are necessary, not just one.

Still, there are many types of people who never did any good deeds. They were experienced in doing bad deeds, right from the start. Because they have many layers of bad karma, they will not be liberated by this, although they are shown and given these objects to think about so many times. Now, if the entrance to the womb has not yet been closed, there are instructions for how to choose which entrance should be chosen. One must ask the Buddhas and Bodhisattvas for help, and repeat the refuge[61] and call the deceased by name three times and say the following:

"Oh noble child [INSERT NAME]! You are dead, now listen. Even though you have been shown with the teachings said above many times, you have not understood them. Now, if the entrance to the womb has not been closed, it is time to choose a body. There is not only one instruction for choosing an entrance to a womb; there are many true and meaningful instructions. Understand and don't let yourself be distracted. Listen closely, concentrate deeply, and you will understand.

"Oh noble child! The signs and traits of the place where you will be born will appear, so recognize them. Look closely at where you will be born and choose the human continent on which you want to be born.

"If you are going to be born in the eastern continent, the Noble Figure[62], you will see a lake that has geese and ganders. Resist the place. Do not go there. Although it is a happy and easy place, dharma is not strong there, so do not go there.

"If you are going to be born in the southern continent, Rose-Apple Island[63], you will see beautiful and grand mansions. You should go there.

"If you are going to be born in the western continent, Enjoyment of Wishfulfilling Cows[64], you will see a lake that is surrounded by male and female horses. Do not go there, but come back here. It is a place of great pleasure, but dharma doesn't blossom there, so don't enter it.

"If you are going to be born in the northern continent, Unpleasant Sound[65], you will see a lake that is surrounded by cows or trees. Recognize that these are signs of taking birth, and do not enter. Although the length of life here is long, and there are many advantages to living here, dharma doesn't flourish here, so don't enter.

"If you are going to be born as a deva, you'll see many beautiful high temples, covered with jewels. If you may enter here, then you should. If you are going to be born as a jealous deity, you'll see many beautiful forests, or what looks like turning wheels of fire. Don't enter here at all and think thoughts to repel and resist.

"If you are going to be born as an animal, you'll see caves in rocks and holes in the ground and huts made of straw. You'll see these images as though through a mist, and if you can, do not enter. If you are going to be born as a hungry ghost, you'll see wasted forests and black shapes protruding form the ground. You'll see shallow caves and patches of blackness. If you go here, you'll be born a hungry ghost, and you experience the misery of hunger and thirst. Don't go here at all, but think powerful thoughts to repel and resist.

"If you are going to be born as a creature from hell, you'll hear wailing songs sung by people with bad karma, or you will have to enter without resistance, or you will feel as though you are in a gloomy land, filled with black and red houses, deep black holes in the earth, and black roads. If you enter here, you will enter hell. You will suffer unbearable pain of terrible heat and terrible cold, and you will never leave. Do not go into that. Do not enter it all. Be very careful. There is a saying: 'Close the entrance to the womb and think about resisting.' That is what is needed now.

"Oh noble child! Even though you don't wish to go, you are powerless. You are being chased by furious karma. You are being dragged by avengers and killers. All around you is darkness. Hurricanes, terrible storms, noise, snow, rain, terrible hailstorms and snowstorms are swirling around you. You will think of escaping from them. You will seek a shelter in your escape, and you will go to the beautiful mansions or caves or holes in the ground, between trees or in the round holes of lotus flowers. You will hide there and you will be afraid. You'll think to yourself, 'I can't leave, now!' and because of your fear of leaving, you'll become very connected to the place in which you are hiding. You are afraid of what is outside in the bardo. You are terrified of them. So, instead of going outside, you will take a body—it doesn't even matter to you if it is a bad body—and you will experience all types of suffering."

This indicates that evil spirits and demons are

interfering with you now. There is a profound teaching for this time, so listen and understand.

"At this moment, when you are terrified and being chased by avengers, you should visualize—immediately and with all of your mind—the Blessed Supreme Heruka or Hayagriva or Vajrapani, or your yidam, if you have one. Imagine it with a huge body and with massive limbs. Imagine that it is angry, furious in its appearance, and that it is able to destroy and evil forces and reduce them to dust. With this figure's blessings and power of grace, you will be separated from the tormenting furies and have the power to choose the entrance to the womb you want. This is the true and meaningful secret of the teaching, so understand it thoroughly.

"Oh noble child! The deities of meditation and other deities are born through the strength of samadhi. Hungry ghosts and many other types of evil spirits have changed their attitudes while in the bardo state, and so they can appear in various imagined forms, as hungry ghosts or demons, and become the mental body itself.

"The hungry ghosts that live deep in the sea and the hungry ghosts that fly through space, all the eighty thousand types of negatives forces, etc., changed their attitude while in the mental body of the bardo. The best thing to do at this time is to think about the Great Symbol about emptiness, but if you can't do that, then think about any image or illusion at all. If you can't do this, then at least do not allow yourself to be attracted by anything. Meditate on the yidam, think about the Great Lord of Compassion, and you will become a Sambhogakaya Buddha in the bardo state.

"Oh noble child! If, because of the power of karma, you have to enter a womb, then the teaching for how to choose a womb is now going to be explained. Listen!

"Do not enter just any womb entrance. If the avengers arrive and you are forced to enter a womb, meditate on Hayagriva. Since you now have some supernatural powers of foresight, you will already know all of the places of birth, one after another. Make your choice accordingly. There are two types of instruction. One is to be transferred into a state of pure Buddha and the other is to choose an impure, samsaric entrance to a womb."

In order to transfer into the state of pure Buddha, direct your imagined projections in the following manner:

“Oh! It is so sad that I am still in this muddy swamp of samsara. Now, even after such a long time, such an endlessly long time, a time without any beginning or end, and while so many other people have already become Buddhas. I am still not liberated. From now on, I am sick of the samsara. It disgusts me and horrifies me. I am totally exhausted by it. Now is the time to run away from it. I must act on my own to be born in a lotus flower at the feet of the Buddha Amitabha, from the red Western Realm of The Blissful.’ Think about this intensely, think about the Blissful Realm of the West. It is crucial that you do this. Alternatively, you can concentrate completely and without distraction on another realm, whatever realm you want—the Pure Realm or the Realm of Complete Joy or the Realm of Willow Leaves or the Palm-tree Mountain or the Palace of Lotus Light in Urgyan. Whatever realm you think about, you will be born into that realm.

“Or, if you wish to be born into the presence of Maitreya in the Joyful Realm, you can think the following thought: ‘The time has come for me now, at this moment in the bardo state, to be in the presence of the Dharma King Maitreya in the Joyful Realm, and so I will go there.’ And then you will be born in the heart of the lotus near Maitreya.

"On the other hand, if you cannot do this, or if you want to enter a womb, or if you have to enter a womb, there is a teaching for choosing an impure, samsaric entrance to a womb, so listen.

"As before, use your supernatural powers of foresight to look at the continent you plan to choose, and enter a place that is rich in dharma.

"If you are going to be born in a dirty pile of garbage, the filth will smell sweetly to you, and you will be attracted to it, and you will be born there. So, don't trust things by how they appear. Do not allow yourself to be attracted or repelled, but choose an entrance to a womb.

"In this situation, also, it is very important to concentrate, by thinking the following thoughts: 'I will be born as a king that is concerned with the good of all human beings, or as a Brahmin[66], like a great sala tree, or as the son of someone who is siddhic[67], or in a family with excellent ancestry, or in a family where both the father and the mother have faith. By being born in a body that has advantages, I can benefit all human beings, and I can do good in the world."

By concentrating on these thoughts, you can enter

the womb. At the same moment, you should bless the womb you are entering, transforming into a palace of the deities. You should plead with the Buddhas and Bodhisattvas of the ten directions and the yidams, especially the Lord of Great Compassion, and enter the womb with a desire of a request for spiritual transference.

"It is possible to make a mistake at this point, by mistaking a bad womb entrance for a good womb, or vice versa. This may occur due to the influence of karma. Again, the main point of this teaching is important, so do the following: Even if the entrance to the womb appears good, do not trust it. At the same time, even if the entrance to the womb appears bad, do not reject it. The ultimate secret is to enter the supreme state in a mood of total impartiality, in which there is neither good nor bad, neither acceptance nor rejection, neither desire nor violent anger.

However, except for those few people who have had experience in this, it is hard to get rid of this disease of unconscious inclinations. If one cannot resist desire and violent, angry behavior in this way, one should call the dead person by name, and say the following words, in order to stop him from seeking shelter with the worst sorts of sinners, with people who are, like beasts, the lowest of the low.

"Oh noble child! If you don't know how to choose an entrance to a womb, and if you cannot get rid of your desires and violent behaviors, regardless of whether the visions described above have appeared, then call upon the Three Jewels and seek shelter in them. Plead with the Lord of Great Compassionate. Walk with your head upright. Give up any attachments or longings you have towards people you have left behind, towards your children, towards friends, towards relatives. They can't help you now. Enter now into the path of the blue light of human beings, the path of the white light of the deities. Enter the palaces of jewels and the gardens of pleasure."

Repeat the following seven times. Then, one should offer the following to Buddhas and Bodhisattvas. Read **The Bardo Prayer which Protects from Fear**, **The Main Verses of the Bardo**, and **Deliverance from the Dangerous Path of the Bardo** up to seven times. Then one should read **The Liberation through Wearing which Spontaneously Liberates the Skandhas**, and **The Daily Practice which Spontaneously Liberates the Unconscious Tendencies**. All of these should be read clearly and distinctly.

By reading these things properly, yogins who have the highest level of insight can cause consciousness to be released during the bardo of the moment of death. They will not have to wander in the bardo state at all. They bypass it right away and are liberated. Below them are few people with some insight and experience; these people will recognize the light of the dharmata after the bardo of the moment before death. They will bypass it and become Buddhas.

Below them are people who will be liberated according to their individual abilities, and in connection with the appearance of one or another peaceful or angry images that are projected in their minds during the bardo of dharmata in the weeks following the moment of death. Because there are many stages, they will recognize whichever stage is appropriate to them, and in this manner become liberated.

However, those who are very weak in good karma, people who face great obstacles because of their very bad karma, will have to wander onward and onward, down the bardo of becoming. However, because there are many exposures, just as there are many steps in a ladder, they will recognize at one step or another, and then they will be liberated.

Still, there may be those whose good karma is very weak, those who do not recognize during any of the stages described above. These people will be awed by terror and fear. For them, there is a series of teachings for how to close the entrance to the womb, or how to choose a womb entrance. This should allow them to recognize one or another, and hopefully achieve the highest degree of virtue for their own situation.

Even the lowest of these people, even if they are similar to beasts, will be rejected from the lowest realm if they seek shelter. Even these people can achieve a wonderful human body—a body full of freedom and good luck—and have the opportunity of meeting a holy teacher, a spiritual friend, in their next life, giving them a chance to be instructed and liberated.

If these instructions are received during the bardo of becoming, it is like putting a pipe in a broken water channel and can succeed in extending a person's good karma.

Even the greatest of sinners can be liberated when they hear these instructions. Why is this? During the bardo, invitations of all are heard at the same time. That is, there are compassionate invitations from the peaceful and angry Buddhas and deities, as well as invitations from the tempting and negative forces.

Just by hearing the instructions at this time, one's attitude is influenced and one is liberated. It is easy to be influenced, because the mental body has no base in blood or flesh.

Regardless of how far they have wandered in the bardo state, they have some karmic supernatural powers of foresight, and with these they can see and hear. These powers are extremely helpful—as soon as they understand, their minds are immediately influenced. It is like a catapult. It is like a huge wooden tree that can't be moved by even a hundred men but, once on water, can be floated in any direction one wants. It is like controlling a horse with reins.

For these reasons, everyone who has died should be approached. If there is a body present, someone should read this reminder over and over again until blood and pus come out of the nostrils. While this is being said, the body should not be moved. The rules to be followed at this time are as follows:

Animals should not be sacrificed for the deceased. Relatives and friends should not cry, mourn or make any noise in front of the deceased. If they need to do this, it can be done somewhere else. Indeed, the family should do as many good deeds as possible during this time.

It is also good to read any other teachings, in addition to **The Great Liberation through Hearing**, at the end of the teaching. It should be read nonstop, over and over again, learnt by heart, and understood. When death is certain and when the signs of death are clear, one should read it aloud to oneself, if one is able, and think about it. If one cannot read it to oneself, it should be given to a dharma brother or dharma sister to read, for it will definitely liberate, there is no doubt about that.

These instructions do not need any practice. It is a profound teaching that liberates just by being seen, heard, read. Even great sinners can be led along the secret path with these meaningful teachings. If one can remember these teachings, even when one is being chased by the seven dogs, one will be liberated in the bardo of the moment before death. Even if all of the Buddhas of all three times—the past, the present and the future—were to search, they wouldn't find a better teaching than this one.

The bardo instruction which liberates human beings, the deep, innermost essence, **The Great Liberation through Hearing**

This treasure was found by the siddha Karma-Lingpa in teh mountain of Gampo-dar. May it benefit the dharma and all sentient beings.

# Sarvamangalam

Inspirational Prayers

A number of texts are connected with **The Great Liberation through Hearing.** They are mentioned in **The Great Liberation through Hearing** as inspirational prayers, and several of them are quoted as part of the instructions to the deceased. The word used to describe these texts is prayer, although they are not prayers in the traditional sense, as they are not actually requests to external deities. Really, they are methods for purifying and directing the mind. The word inspirational is used to describe them because they are meant to inspire the mind by exciting its natural desire for goodness. This, ultimately, enables their purpose to be fulfilled.

## Inspirational Prayer for Rescue to Buddhas and Bodhisattvas

One should always call upon the Buddhas and Bodhisattvas for rescue at the time of death. One should make offerings to the Three Jewels—offerings which are physical and real as well as offerings that are imagined in the mind. One should hold sweet-smelling incense in one's hand and says the following words, with deep concentration:

Oh Buddhas and Bodhisattvas! Who live in all ten directions and who have great compassion and wonderful powers of foresight. Who can see with a divine eye, who have love, who give protection to sentient beings, who come to this lower place due to your great passion and are willing to accept these offerings, both those which tangible and laid out and those which are offered in the mind.

Oh Compassionate Ones! You have deep wisdom of understanding, loving compassion, the power to do remarkable actions and to protect.

Oh Compassionate Ones! This person, [INSERT NAME], is leaving this world. He is going onto another world. He is dying without choice. He is making a great leap and undergoing a great change.

He has no friends. He is miserable. He has no one to protect him and no shelter. He has no family to look out for him, and there is no one to act for his benefit.

In this world, his light has been extinguished. He is now going to another place. He is going into thick darkness, falling down a steep cliff. He is going into a terrible jungle of solitude and loneliness.

He is being chased by karmic forces. He is entering a deep and vast silence. He is being carried away by a great body of water. He is being blown by the winds of karma, traveling where there is no stability, no solid ground. He is starting upon a great conflict, and will soon be engaged in a terrible battle.

He will be overcome by an awful and evil spirit. He is frightened by the messengers that have been sent by the Lord of Death. He is entering one existence after another because of his karma. He is helpless. Now is the time when he must go, alone, without any friends.

Oh Compassionate Ones! Defend [INSERT NAME] because he is defenseless. Protect him, because he has no shelter. Defend him, and save him from the great darkness that is the bardo. Turn him away from the great storm that is karma. Protect him from his awe, terror, and fear of the Lord of Death. Save him from the long and dangerous pathway of the bardo.

Oh Compassionate Ones! Don't offer compassion that is small or weak. Help him! Help him so that he doesn't go into misery, or into the miserable lower states of existence. Don't forget your ancient promises. Don't let your compassion be weak.

Oh Buddhas and Bodhisattvas! Don't let your methods of compassion for [INSERT NAME] be small or weak. Grab him with the hook of your grace and compassion. Don't let a sentient being fall into the power of evil karma.

Oh Three Jewels! Be a shelter for him from suffering in the bardo.

This should be said three times, with great devotion and deep faith, by oneself, and by all others. Then, **The Great Liberation through Hearing**, **Deliverance from the Dangerous Path of the Bardo**, and **The Bardo Prayer which Protects from Fear** should be read.

## The Main Verses of the Six Bardos

Now, as the bardo of birth dawns on me,
I will leave behind idleness,
As there is no time for idleness in life.
I will embark upon the path of study, reflection, and meditation,
And I will not be distracted.
I will project images in my mind,
And follow the path,
And realize the three kayas.
Now that I have achieved a human body,
May there be no time for the mind to wander,
While I am on the path.

Now, as the bardo of dreams dawns on me,
I will leave behind careless ignorance, which is like the sleep of a corpse.
I will allow my consciousness to exist in its natural state,
Without distraction.
Understanding the dreams and training myself,
In the clear light.
I will not sleep like an animal, in slothfulness,
Instead, I will blend together the sleeping state with the experience of being awake.
Now, as the bardo of samadhi-meditation dawns on me,

I will leave behind the mass,
Of distractions and confusions.
I will rest my mind,
In the mood of the endless state,
That has no distractions or disturbances,
May firmness be achieved in both the seeing stage and the perfected stage.
At this moment, while focusing on meditation, and while putting all other activities aside,
I will not be influenced by the power of confused emotions.

Now, as the bardo of the moment before death dawns on me,
I will leave behind all cravings,
All yearnings, all attraction for worldly objects.
I will enter into a state of the clear awareness of the teachings,
Without distraction.
I will transport my consciousness,
into the space of the unborn mind.
When the hour comes for me to leave the body made of flesh and blood,
I will know how it is to be transient and illusory.

Now, as the bardo of the dharmata dawns on me,
I will leave behind all fear, all awe, all terror.
I will recognize everything that appears, As an image that I have projected in my mind,

And I will recognize that it is a vision of the bardo.
Now that I have reached this important hour,
I will not be frightened of the peaceful and angry beings,
In the images I have projected in my own mind.

Now, as the bardo of becoming dawns on me,
I will focus my mind totally,
I will try to extend the effects of good karma,
To close the entrance to the womb,
And think thoughts of resistance.
This is the time,
When I need dedication and pure love.
I must leave behind jealousy, and meditate on the guru and his mate.

By not thinking of the death that is approaching,
And by allowing one's mind to wander,
One's performance of these activities has no meaning.
And one returns without anything except complete confusion.
One must recognize the holy dharma,
So why not practice it,
At this very moment?
Siddahs say the following:
If you don't keep your guru's teachings in your heart,
Aren't you just deceiving yourself?

## Deliverance from the Dangerous Path of the Bardo

I pay respect to the gurus, the yidams and the
dakinis,
Who, with their great love, may lead us on the
path.

When I wander in samsara,
In confusion.
On the focused bright path of study, reflection, and
meditation,
May the sacred gurus lead me,
And may their consorts, the hosts of the dakinis,
Protect me from behind.
May they help me to cross,
The bardo's dangerous path,
And bring me to the perfect Buddha state.

When I wander in samsara,
Due to my great stupidity,
In the path of the shining light,
Of the wisdom of dharmadhatu,
May the Blessed Vairocana lead me,
And may his mate, the Queen of Vajra Space,
Protect me from behind.
May they help me to cross,
The bardo's dangerous path,
And bring me to the perfect Buddha state.

When I wander in samsara,
Due to my great anger,
In the path of the shining light,
Of the wisdom of the image in the mirror,
May the Blessed Vajrasattva lead me,
And may his mate, Buddha-Locana,
Protect me from behind.
May they help me to cross,
The bardo's dangerous path,
And bring me to the perfect Buddha state.

When I wander in samsara,
Due to my intense pride,
In the path of the shining light,
Of the wisdom of equality,
May the Blessed Ratnasambhava lead me,
And may his mate, Mamaki,
Protect me from behind.
May they help me to cross,
The bardo's dangerous path,
And bring me to the perfect Buddha state.

When I wander in samsara,
Due to my strong desire,
In the path of the shining light,
Of the wisdom of discrimination,
May the Blessed Amitabha lead me,
And may his mate, Pandaravasini,

Protect me from behind.
May they help me to cross,
The bardo's dangerous path,
And bring me to the perfect Buddha state.

When I wander in samsara,
Due to my intense envy,
In the path of the shining light,
Of the wisdom of performance,
May the Blessed Amoghasiddhi lead me,
And may his mate, Samaya-Tara,
Protect me from behind.
May they help me to cross,
The bardo's dangerous path,
And bring me to the perfect Buddha state.

When I wander in samsara,
Due to my intense inclinations,
Along the bright path,
Of innate wisdom,
May the vidyadharas and warriors lead me,
And may their mates, the dakinis, be behind me.
And may they help me to cross,
The bardo's dangerous path,
And bring me to the perfect Buddha state.

When I wander in samsara,
Through fierce and confused images that I have
projected from my mind,

On the bright path of leaving behind all fear,
May the Bless Ones, peaceful and angry, lead me,
And may the host of the dakinis, the Queens of Space, go behind me.
And may they help me to cross,
The bardo's dangerous path,
And bring me to the perfect Buddha state.

May supernatural elements not rise up to become my enemies,
And may I see the realm of the blue Buddha.

May watery elements not rise up to become my enemies,
And may I see the realm of the white Buddha.

May earthly elements not rise up to become my enemies,
And may I see the realm of the yellow Buddha.

May fiery elements not rise up to become my enemies,
And may I see the realm of the red Buddha.

May elements of the air not rise up to become my enemies,
And may I see the realm of the green Buddha.

May the elements of the rainbow not rise up to
become my enemies,
And may I see all the realms of all the Buddhas.

May the sounds, lights, and rays not rise up to
become my enemies,
And may I see the limitless realms of the peaceful
ones and the angry ones.

May I recognize that all of the sounds I hear are my
own sounds,
May I recognize all of the lights I see are my own
lights,
May I recognize all of the rays I see are my own
rays.
May I recognize the bardo as myself in a moment,
And may I achieve the realms of the three kayas.

## The Bardo Prayer which Protects from Fear

When my life's journey is over,
And since no relatives can go with me when I leave this world,
I wander in the bardo, all by myself.

May the peaceful and the angry Buddhas,
Send out their compassion,
And may their compassion,
Get rid of the gloom and darkness.

When wandering alone, away from my beloved friends,
The empty forms of the images I project appear,
May the Buddhas send out their powers compassion,
So that the terrors of the bardo do not come.

When the five bright lights of wisdom are shining,
May I recognize that they are from me, and may I not be frightened or scared.

When I suffer due to the power of bad karma,
May the peaceful and angry Buddhas come to clear away my suffering.
When the sound of dharmata roars,
And sounds like a thousand thunders.

May it be transformed into the sound,
Of the instructions of the Mahayana.

When I follow my karma, and when I do not have a shelter,
May the peaceful and angry Buddhas be a shelter for me.
When I suffer the karma of unconscious inclinations,
May the samadhi of happiness and bright arise.
At the moment of spontaneous birth in the bardo of becoming,
May I be blind to the false revelations of the tempters.
When I arrive wherever I want to arrive,
May I knot see the illusory terrors of bad karma.

When there are roars from savage creatures,
May it be changed to the sound of dharma, to the six syllables.
When I am chased by snow, rain, wind, and darkness,
May I see with the clear, divine eye of wisdom.

Let it be that all sentient beings,
Of the same order in the bardo,
Be born into a higher state,
Without any jealousy one toward the other.

When passion causes great thirst and hunger,
May the suffering associated with this thirst and
hunger, and with heat and cold, not be felt.

When I see my parents of the future together,
May I see the peaceful and angry Buddhas with
their mates.
When I have the power to choose where I will be
born,
For the good of others,
May I receive a perfect body,
That is decorated with signs and graces.

When I have obtained a perfect body,
May every person who hears and sees me, Be
liberated right away.
May I never follow bad karma,
May it be that I only follow virtues and good
qualities,
And that they be multiplied.

Wherever I am born,
At that place,
May it be that I meet the yidam of this life,
Face to face,
That I may know how to walk and talk,
As soon as I am born.
May I have the power to remember,
And may I remember my past lives.

In all stages of learning,
High, middle and low,
May I understand just by hearing, thinking, seeing.
May the land be blessed,
Wherever I am born,
So that all sentient beings will be happy.

Oh peaceful and angry Buddhas,
May I and others,
Become like you,
Just as you are,
With your forms and your favorable markings,
With your attendants, your long life, and your
dominions.

Samantabhardra, the peaceful and angry ones,
With infinite compassion,
The power of truth of the pure dharmata,
And followers of tantra in concentrated meditation.
May their blessings fulfill this inspirational prayer.

# Endnotes

[1] **The Liberation through Wearing** is a short text that is tied to the body of the deceased as an amulet. It contains mostly mantras.

[2] Guru means spiritual teacher.

[3] Amitabha is a Buddha believed to have great merits thanks to good deeds conducted over countless past lives.

[4] Dharmakaya is the body of the truth.

[5] Sambhogakaya is the body of mutual enjoyment.

[6] Nirmanakaya is the physical situation.

[7] Bardo is the gap or intermediate stage between two states of existence, between life and rebirth.

[8] Ejection from consciousness is when a person who practices yoga send his awareness toward an imaginary picture in order to direct his consciousness.

[9] Dharmata is the true nature of being.

[10] Yogi is a person skilled in meditation.

[11] As visible from outside.

[12] As evident on the inside.

[13] The Three Jewels, also known as the Three Treasures or the Triple Gem, are as follows: the Buddha, the main source of instruction; the Dhamma, the doctrine based on this instruction; and the Sangha, the community who lives by this doctrine.

[14] A Buddha is one who is awake to the truth, one who has left behind emotions such as anger and desire and has deep wisdom and inner peace. In short, it is someone who has reached enlightenment.

[15] A Bodhisattva is one who is dedicated to assisting others to achieve Buddhahood

[16] The vow of samaya is a vow of commitment made by Buddhas and Bodhisattvas to lead all people to enlightenment.

[17] Prana is the vital, life-sustaining force found in people.

[18] This is the nerve center of the soul, as well.

[19] Awareness in the natural state first.

[20] This occurs after the prana crosses over the central nerves of the navel.

[21] Twenty or thirty minutes, approximately.

[22] This is the position in which Gautama Buddha lay at his death. He was stretched out on the right side, with his right hand under the head.

[23] Brahmarandhra is a spot on the head connected by a cord in the spinal column with the heart.

[24] Sutras are records of the oral teachings of Gautama Buddha.

[25] Tantras are considered very high (or even the highest) teachings of Tibetan Buddhism.

[26] Sentient beings are enlightened beings devoted to the liberation of others.

[27] The Great Symbol is a meditation practice which produces a state of great happiness from the union of male and female aspects.

[28] Samantabhardri is the female mate of Samantabhardra.

[29] Samantabhardra represents the practice and meditation of all Buddhas

[30] In the Completion Stage, everything dissolves into emptiness and shapelessness.

[31] In the Generation Stage, the yogi imagines the four purities and identifies with them.

[32] Sandhana is a meditation exercise.

[33] Yidam is a deity that represents the enlightened nature of a student. It is generally picked by a guru in order to suit his plans and practices.

[34] The Pure Illusory Body is the unearthly counterpart of the physical body.

[35] The Illumination of the Mother is the basis and natural state of each person.

[36] The Illumination of the Son is the true nature of consciousness.

[37] Samadhi is the state in which one is aware of one's existence without thinking. Samadhi-meditation is a practice that leads to complete meditation.

[38] Samsara is recurring rebirth filled with suffering and problems.

[39] Five skandhas are necessary for creating an individual.

[40] Dharmadhatu is the realm of the dharma, the collection of all dharma.

[41] Devas are exalted beings who live in various realms as rewards for good deeds.

[42] Vajra is a weapon shaped like a thunderbolt.

[43] Shang-shang birds are mythological birds that have a human torso.

[44] Mandala is landscape of the Buddha land. They are often used to aid in meditation.

[45] Dharma is the natural law, reality, or the way of natural truths.

[46] A Vidyadhara is a holder of knowledge.

[47] Dakinis, literally translated as sky dancers, are supernatural female beings that act as muses in spiritual practice.

[48] A tantric yogin is an individual who practices tantra as a method for self-realization.

[49] The Great Complete is a stage in meditation that penetrates beyond the vision of the Great Symbol, into an experience of openness and formlessness.

[50] Heruka represents indivisible bliss and emptiness. The Glorious Great Buddha-Heruka is a combination of the Buddha-Heruka and the Great Heruka. The Great Heruka is the origin of the herukas of the five families.

[51] A Garuda is a mythical bird, similar to a horned eagle. It is usually depicted with a partially human form.

[52] Gauris, referred to in other texts as Kerimas, are goddesses believed to have human shape.

[53] Picasis, referred to in other texts as Htamenma, are goddesses believed to have human bodies and animal heads.

[54] Yoginis, referred to in other texts as Wang-chugma, are goddesses believed to have human bodies and animal heads.

[55] A goad is a pointed rod used to urge on animals.

[56] Mount Meru is a sacred mountain in Buddhist mythology. It is considered to be the center of the universe.

[57] The vajra seat is the seat on which Gautama Buddha sat when he was enlightened at Bodhgaya.

[58] A stupa is a spiritual monument that represents the Buddha's body, his speech and his mind.

[59] Sangha is the association or assembly, a group of beings possessing some degree of enlightenment.

[60] Gandharvas are deities believed to live in the sky or atmosphere.

[61] Refuge in this context refers to the formal commitment to the Buddhist path.

[62] The Noble Figure is known in other texts as the Purva-Videha.

[63] Rose-Apple Island is known in other texts as Jambu Island.

[64] Enjoyment of Wishfulfilling Cows is known in other texts as Apara-Godarniya.

[65] Unpleasant Sound is known in other texts as Kuru.

[66] Brahmin are a social class considered responsible for society's spiritual elements.

[67] Siddhic is a person accomplished in self-awareness and enlightenment.